LAVINGTON & DEVIZES
MOTOR SERVICES

LAVINGTON & DEVIZES
MOTOR SERVICES

Laurie James

AMBERLEY

First published 2014

Amberley Publishing
The Hill, Stroud
Gloucestershire, GL5 4EP

www.amberley-books.com

Copyright © Laurie James 2014

The right of Laurie James to be identified as the Author
of this work has been asserted in accordance with the
Copyrights, Designs and Patents Act 1988.

All rights reserved. No part of this book may be reprinted
or reproduced or utilised in any form or by any electronic,
mechanical or other means, now known or hereafter invented,
including photocopying and recording, or in any information
storage or retrieval system, without the permission in writing
from the Publishers.

British Library Cataloguing in Publication Data.
A catalogue record for this book is available from the British Library.

ISBN 978 1 4456 3918 5 (print)
ISBN 978 1 4456 3929 1 (ebook)

Typeset in 10pt on 12pt Sabon.
Typesetting and Origination by Amberley Publishing.
Printed in the UK.

Contents

Acknowledgements	7
Preface	9
Introduction	11
The Horse Era	15
The Motor Bus Arrives	21
Post-War Recovery	31
Boundaries and Opportunities	37
Preparing for Further Growth	43
Moving South – Halls of Orcheston	49
The Heyday of the Company	53
A Downward Slide	67
Legislation and Consolidation	77
Under New Ownership	85
Submersion into the Tilling Group	97
Afterwards: A Selective Miscellany	103
Map of Lavington & Devizes Motor Services Bus Routes	118
Appendix 1: Bus Services of F. H. Sayer and Lavington & Devizes Motor Services Ltd 1915–37	119
Appendix 2: List of Vehicles Known to Have Been Operated by Lavington & Devizes Motor Services	123
Bibliography	128

Lavington & Devizes Motor Services

410A—410C] NOTE—LIGHT FIGURES FROM 1201 A.M. TO 1200 NOON / HEAVY DARK FIGURES FROM 1201 P.M. TO 1200 MIDNIGHT **[410A—410C**

LAVINGTON & DEVIZES MOTOR SERVICE, LTD.

410A — DEVIZES AND PEWSEY

DOWN — THURS. & SATS. / SO / THURS., SATS. AND SUNS. ONLY / SUNS.

	THURS. & SATS.			SUNS.		UP THURS. & SATS.		SUNS.
DEVIZES	945	300	830	230	700	↑1215 530	—	515 945
HORTON	1000	315	845	245	715	1200 515	—	500 930
ALL CANNINGS	1015	330	900	300	730	1145 500	—	445 915
ALTON BARNES	1025	340	910	310	740	1135 450	—	435 905
WOODBOROUGH	1030	345	915	315	745	1130 445	—	430 900
HILCOTT	1035	350	920	320	750	1125 440	—	425 855
NORTH NEWNTON	1040	355	925	325	755	1120 435	—	420 850
WOODBRIDGE	1045	400	930	330	800	1115 430	—	415 845
MANNINGFORD BRUCE	1050	405	935	335	805	1110 425	—	410 840
PEWSEY	1100	415	945	345	815↓	1100 415	—	400 830

SO SATS. ONLY

410B — SALISBURY, SHREWTON AND ORCHESTON AND DEVIZES

WEEKDAYS (Tu / SO / SX / SO / SX SO) — **SUNDAYS**

SALISBURY	915	1200	200	300	400	430	530	830	845	1030	200	600 800 1000
WILTON	930	1215	215	315	415	445	545	845	900	1045	215	615 815 1015
SOUTH NEWTON	935	1225	220	320	425	450	550	850	905	1050	220	620 820 1020
STOFORD	940	1230	225	325	430	455	555	855	910	1055	225	625 825 1025
STAPLEFORD	945	1240	230	330	440	500	600	900	915	1100	230	630 830 1030
BERWICK ST. JAMES	950	1245	240	335	445	505	605	910	920	1110	235	635 835 1035
WINTERBOURNE STOKE	955	1250	250	340	450	515	615	915	930	1120	240	640 840 1040
SHREWTON	1005	110	300	355	505	530	630	930	945	1135	250	700 850 1050
ORCHESTON ST. GEORGE	—	120	—	—	—	—	—	—	—	1145	—	—
TILSHEAD	1020	—	—	405	—	—	C 640	945	—	—	305	— 905 —
GORE CROSS	1030	—	—	415	—	—	C 650	955	—	—	315	— 915 —
WEST LAVINGTON	1040	—	—	420	—	—	C 700	1005	—	—	325	— 925 —
MARKET LAVINGTON	—	—	—	—	—	—	—	1010	—	—	100	— — —
LITTLETON PANNELL	1050	—	—	425	—	—	C 705	—	—	—	110	335 935 —
BLACK DOG	1055	—	—	432	—	—	C 715	—	—	—	115	340 940 —
POTTERNE WICK	1100	—	—	440	—	—	C 720	—	—	—	120	345 945 —
POTTERNE	1103	—	—	445	—	—	C 723	—	—	—	123	348 948 —
DEVIZES	1115	—	—	500	—	—	C 735	—	—	—	130	400 1000 —

WEEKDAYS (TS / SX / SX SO / SO / SO) — **SUNDAYS**

DEVIZES	—	900	—	315	—	—	530	1015	—	130	— 800 1000 —
POTTERNE	—	910	—	325	—	—	540	1025	—	140	— 810 1010 —
POTTERNE WICK	—	913	—	328	—	—	543	1030	—	143	— 813 1013 —
BLACK DOG	—	918	—	333	—	—	548	1040	—	148	— 818 1018 —
LITTLETON PANNELL	—	923	—	338	—	—	553	1050	—	153	— 823 1023 —
MARKET LAVINGTON	—	—	—	—	—	—	—	—	—	—	— 1028 —
WEST LAVINGTON	—	928	—	343	—	—	558	1100	—	158	— 828 —
GORE CROSS	—	938	—	353	—	—	608	1110	—	208	— 838 —
TILSHEAD	—	948	—	403	—	—	618	1120	—	218	— 848 —
ORCHESTON ST. GEORGE	745	930	—	120	—	—	545	—	1245	—	— — —
SHREWTON	755	945	1000	130	300	415	530	600	640	1135	100	230 700 900
WINTERBOURNE STOKE	805	1000	1015	145	315	435	545	615	650	—	115	245 715 915
BERWICK ST. JAMES	810	1005	1020	150	320	435	550	620	700	—	120	250 720 920
STAPLEFORD	815	1010	1025	155	325	440	600	625	710	—	125	255 725 925
STOFORD	820	1015	1030	200	330	445	605	630	715	—	130	300 730 930
SOUTH NEWTON	825	1020	1035	205	335	450	610	635	720	—	135	305 735 935
WILTON	830	1030	1045	215	340	500	615	645	735	—	145	315 745 945
SALISBURY	845	1045	1100	230	400	515	630	700	755	—	200	330 800 1000

C OR SO SATS. ONLY.   SX NOT SATS.   TO THURS. ONLY.   TS TUES. AND SATS. ONLY.   Tu TUES. ONLY

410C — MARKET LAVINGTON, DEVIZES, MELKSHAM, BOX AND BATH

MONS., TUES., WEDS. & FRIS. — **THURS.** — **SATS.** — **SUNS.**

MARKET LAVINGTON	—	900	200	420	900	—	—	900	200	—	530	130	— 730 — —
POTTERNE	—	920	225	445	920	—	—	920	225	—	555	145	— — — —
DEVIZES	—	940	245	505	940	1012	300	415	940	245	—	645	210 415 815 — —
SEEND	—	955	300	520	955	1027	315	430	955	300	—	700	230 430 850 —
MELKSHAM	—	1010	315	535	1010	1042	330	445	1010	305	615	715	240 445 845 —
ATWORTH	—	1030	335	555	1030	—	—	505	1030	335	635	735	255 500 900 —
BOX	—	1045	350	610	1045	—	—	520	1045	350	650	750	310 515 915 —
BATH	—	1110	410	630	1110	—	—	545	1110	410	718	820	340 540 940 —

MONS., TUES., WEDS. & FRIS. — **THURS.** — **SATS.** — **SUNS.**

BATH	—	230	500	700	845	—	—	500	1230	500	800	930	230 630 800 — —
BOX	—	255	525	725	910	—	—	525	1255	525	825	955	255 656 825 — —
ATWORTH	—	310	540	740	925	—	—	540	110	540	840	1010	310 710 840 — —
MELKSHAM	—	325	600	800	940	1045	330	600	130	600	900	1030	325 725 856 — —
SEEND	—	340	615	805	955	1100	345	615	140	615	—	1040	340 740 910 — —
DEVIZES	—	355	630	830	1010	1115	400	630	200	630	—	1100	355 755 930 — —
POTTERNE	—	445	640	840	—	—	—	640	315	640	—	1115	— 845 950 — —
MARKET LAVINGTON	—	520	710	910	—	—	—	710	345	710	—	1135	— 910 1010 — —

856

L&DMS services 410A–C from the spring 1931 *Roadway* timetable booklet.

Acknowledgements

Over many years, Roger Grimley, noted historian of many small bus operators in the West Country, collected much source material on Lavington & Devizes Motor Services and the company's owners, including bus service records, notes on vehicles and other background information. He suggested I use his large file of papers to produce a book, supplemented by considerable additional research, which has now been carried out, using archive sources and local enquiries. What you are about to read is firmly based on Roger's detective work and I am extremely grateful to him for generously sharing his material.

Two other stalwart researchers, supporters, illustration providers and advisors have been Dr John Batten and Roger Frost, the curator of Market Lavington Museum. Roger runs an excellent daily blog on the museum's website, sometimes turning up new photographs and information of local events long past; he has facilitated the use of many images from the museum's collection and has investigated queries. Before him, the late Peggy Gye collected many of the photographs.

Others have facilitated research, passed on notes or memories or provided photographs – Peter Jaques of the Kithead Trust, Andrew Waller, David Pennels, Lionel Tancock, Peter Daniels, Derek Persson, Steve Chislett, Geoff Lusher, Mike Wadman, Michael Gale of Devizes, Pat Hale of Market Lavington and the late Geoff Bruce. My sincere gratitude goes to all of them and to Roger Atkinson and John King who have provided tickets from their collections.

I must also acknowledge input and assistance from Bath City Records Office, Bristol Records Office, Devizes Library, the Omnibus Society Library at Walsall, the PSV Circle, the Wiltshire & Swindon History Centre at Chippenham and various websites – Census 1911, Commercial Motor Archive, Devizes Heritage, Historical Directories and Market Lavington Museum.

At the back of the book is a selected bibliography for titles which have been consulted to varying degrees and information extracted. I am indebted to all the authors, compilers and publishers. Images of Lavington & Devizes vehicles are not particularly plentiful and sometimes lacking in the quality or variety that one would ideally like. Many of the charabanc images in Salisbury were captured by Harold Whitworth, but it is not known who actually originated most of the others used in the book, so in general they are credited to the supplying source. In this context, the abbreviation MLM refers to the Market Lavington Museum Collection. Apologies are sincerely offered if any photographs are inadvertently incorrectly attributed.

Finally, as always, but in no way least, love and gratitude to my wife Michaela for her IT skills, support and tolerance.

The events described are mainly of 80 to 100 years ago and establishing the correct version of events is often frustrated by the lack of, or conflict in, documentary or photographic evidence. Much has been lost in the mists of time and now we will probably never know. As always, any error of interpretation or omission is mine alone and I apologise if I have inadvertently conveyed or perpetuated a falsehood. Efforts to locate any surviving descendants of Fred Sayer have not been fruitful, so if any see this, I would be delighted if they got in contact.

Laurie James, Walton on Thames, 2014

Preface

Lavington & Devizes Motor Services (L&DMS) was not a typical West Country rural independent bus operator. Across Britain, many village-based concerns made the gradual transition from carrier to running buses and coaches, with many of those originally using horses progressing to motorised propulsion either just before, during or after the end of the First World War. In general, they ran one or a few modest services to the nearest town(s), often only on popular days such as that when the market was held. However, in contrast, L&DMS quickly established from 1920 a daily network of bus services across a large part of central and west Wiltshire, where major undertakings were slow to develop, with an unusually large fleet of buses and charabancs. The firm's founder – Fred Sayer – had been driving buses (and possibly trams) since the mid-1900s, a time when motor omnibuses were in their infancy. Mechanical skills, no doubt learned the hard way from necessity, would stand him in good stead when he started his own business.

Fred's motor engineering expertise and his business acumen made him something of an entrepreneur whose expanding operations attracted interest from wealthy local investors. This was at a time when country folk were broadening their horizons in terms of needing to travel locally and also taking the opportunity of the new-found desire and ability to enjoy affordable pleasure trips to the coast and countryside by charabanc. Yet, even by mid-1920s standards, Sayer's vehicles were somewhat antiquated, using chassis acquired cheaply after military use or made from parts of other vehicles, enhanced by components supplied in kit form by manufacturers such as AEC. Nevertheless, by the end of that decade, economies were needed and there was only a limited financial ability to update the fleet with more modern and attractive vehicles. Attempts to cut losses and sell the company did not reach fruition until 1932, by which time it was in poor financial shape. The buyer was a long-established concern based in Bath – an undertaking that had provided employment for Fred Sayer before he ran his own business and one that had exercised influence on his activities and his operating area in various ways.

L&DMS was certainly an interesting early operator, a pioneer in some respects, only touched on to date in published transport histories. This book sets out to remedy that omission, as we turn the clock back 100 years and more, to the dawn of motorised passenger transport in the Wiltshire town of Devizes and the village of Market Lavington. The story is as much about changes in the way of life as it is about the developing bus industry in rural Wiltshire.

This enamel double-sided sign once hung outside an L&DMS agent's premises, or perhaps one of the company's own offices. It was discovered in good condition in a shed at Easterton Sands as recently as June 2014. (R. Frost)

Introduction

The pleasant large village of Market Lavington is situated in a fertile valley at the foot of the north-western scarp slope of the chalk massif known as Salisbury Plain. This has earned it the soubriquet of 'Village under the Plain'. Through time it has been known variously as Chepyng Lavington, Steeple Lavington and East Lavington, before its present name persisted. It is 90 miles from London, 10 miles from Westbury, 19 miles north-west of Salisbury and 5 miles south-east from Devizes. To the north of the village centre, the soil is of Gault clay, rising to a ridge of Upper Greensand, known, appropriately, as The Sands. In the eighteenth century, this sandy soil led to the development of orchards and market gardening. The clay provided material for brick making until the 1950s. At one time there were significant malting and brewing activities, but the last local establishment to brew its own beer was, again appropriately, The Brewery Tap in around 1920. The Devizes to Salisbury road went through Market Lavington and then over The Plain until 1899 but this was then diverted through West Lavington; between 1897 and 1911, 2,000 acres of mainly farmland in the parish of Market Lavington were taken over by the War Department for military training purposes, such as artillery ranges. Several large camps were established around The Plain.

In the thirteenth century, two families owned the manorial land and Richard Rochelle, whose family had title to the land in the centre of the village, was granted a market charter in 1254. There is still a Market Place – albeit much changed since the period when it was of significance to this story – but the last Wednesday markets were held there in the 1850s, as such activities had been usurped by Devizes over a long period.

The Great Western Railway arrived late in the vicinity of Market Lavington. It was not until 29 July 1900 that Lavington station opened for goods, and 1 October that year for passengers. It was actually in Littleton Panell and was on a new main line from Patney & Chirton Junction to Westbury. However, Devizes station was on a line between Patney & Chirton and Holt Junction, which opened in 1857, once part of a through route from London and Newbury to Bristol. The railway through Devizes closed on 18 April 1966, the same day as Lavington station. Trains still roar through

As he did innumerable times in the 1920s and 1930s, Salisbury photographer Harold Whitworth captured this Market Lavington charabanc party on film during the morning comfort stop en route to the coast, and then sold copies to the passengers during the evening break. Sitting to the right of the driver could be Fred Sayer, the principal of L&DMS, while the vicar of Market Lavington from 1906 to 1940, Revd John Sturton, accompanies the party with his BSA motorcycle and sidecar. (MLM)

the latter on their way from London to Westbury, Taunton and beyond, although little evidence remains of the station. Market Lavington's first regular local public road transport in the 1870s linked to Devizes, as the railhead at that time.

At 400 feet above sea level, Devizes has been described as a 'solid, respectable market town' in central Wiltshire, with apparently one of the largest market squares in the west of England. Its name is said to come from the Latin *ad divisas*, or meeting point on several boundaries – in this case the manors of Potterne, Rowde and Bishops Cannings. Main roads radiate out to all points of the compass; in the historic town centre, some structures survive from the sixteenth century and there are a number of notable and imposing buildings from the Georgian era.

The Kennet & Avon Canal, completed in 1810, runs through Devizes, forming part of an inland navigation from the River Thames at Reading comprising the canalised River Kennet to Newbury, a canal to Bath and then the River Avon onwards to Bristol and Avonmouth at the Bristol Channel. Just outside of the town is the famous series of twenty-nine locks, including a spectacular run of sixteen in a staircase at Caen Hill. After the opening of the Great Western Railway, the canal's fortunes waned and it gradually fell into disuse over a long period and became derelict. Slowly restored, re-instatement of the navigation from Reading to Bath was finally completed in 1990 for leisure purposes.

As a thriving commercial centre with many trades, shops and the large Thursday market, Devizes provided those things not available in smaller settlements. It was also a place to sell local produce and to buy and sell farm commodities. Transport needs for goods gave rise to a proliferation of carriers, whose horse-drawn wagons and vans came in on market days and sometimes on other days from virtually every village in the surrounding area. During the day, these would be stabled either in the marketplace itself or in the yards of various inns. Some of these carriers made the transition to the motor vehicle from about 1912 onwards and some reinvented themselves as bus operators, as in many other rural parts of the UK. A number of bus services coming in from surrounding villages only ran on the most popular days – Thursdays and Saturdays. Many people worked until lunchtime on Saturday and then received their weekly wages, before taking the bus to town. Shops would stay open until later in the evening, sometimes selling off perishable goods at bargain prices to those on low incomes. There was also evening entertainment to be had, either in one of the numerous public houses or at the cinema. Finally, on Saturday evenings there was the culinary treat of Mrs Tippett's whelk stall to be sampled while waiting for the bus back home from near the Pelican Inn in Devizes' marketplace.

A carrier from Market Lavington ran a horse-drawn omnibus as early as the 1870s, but it was left to outsiders to develop motor bus services from the village, as this account will attempt to describe.

110D — 410E] NOTE—LIGHT FIGURES FROM 1201 A.M. TO 1200 NOON. HEAVY DARK FIGURES FROM 1201 P.M. TO 1200 MIDNIGHT **[410D — 410E**

LAVINGTON & DEVIZES MOTOR SERVICE, LTD.—*continued.*

410D — MARKET LAVINGTON, EDINGTON, MELKSHAM AND BATH

WEDS. AND SATS. ONLY

DOWN WEDS. SATS.		UP WEDS. SATS.
830 145	MARKET LAVINGTON	830 1045
845 200	ERLESTOKE	815 1030
855 210	TINHEAD	805 1020
900 215	EDINGTON	800 1015
910 225	BRATTON	750 1005
920 235	STEEPLE ASHTON	740 955
940 255	KEEVIL	720 935
950 305	SEMINGTON	710 925
1000 315	MELKSHAM	700 915
1030 335	ATWORTH	640 855
1045 350	BOX	625 840
1110 410	BATH	600 815

410E — MARKET LAVINGTON AND DEVIZES

MONS., TUES., FRIS. AND SATS.

	SO			SO	SO	SO			SO	SO	SO	SO			
MARKET LAVINGTON	800	830	900	1000	..	1100	1200	100	200	400	420	530	630	..	730	..
WEST LAVINGTON	807	..	..	1007	1040	1107	..	..	207	407	..	537	637	700	737	..
LITTLETON PANELL	810	835	905	1015	1043	1115	1210	110	210	410	425	540	640	703	740	..
GREAT CHEVERELL RD.	815	838	910	1020	1048	1120	1215	115	215	415	430	545	645	708	745	..
BLACK DOG	820	840	913	1025	1055	1125	1220	120	220	420	432	550	650	713	750	..
POTTERNE WICK	825	845	918	1030	1100	1130	1225	125	225	425	440	555	655	718	755	..
POTTERNE	830	848	920	1035	1103	1135	1230	130	230	430	445	600	700	723	800	..
POTTERNE BUTTS	833	850	925	1040	1105	1140	1233	133	233	433	447	603	703	726	803	..
MOUNT PLEASANT	835	852	930	1045	1107	1145	1235	135	235	435	450	605	705	728	808	..
DEVIZES	845	900	940	1050	1110	1150	1245	145	245	445	500	610	710	738	813	..

WEDNESDAYS — **THURSDAYS**

MARKET LAVINGTON	800	900	..	200	420	800	..	900	1000	..	1100	1200	1230	100	130	300	400	500
WEST LAVINGTON	..	..	1050	..	..	807	..	1000	1040	..	..	1237	..	137	307	407	507
LITTLETON PANELL	810	905	1053	210	425	810	903	1010	1043	1110	1210	1240	110	140	310	410	510
GREAT CHEVERELL RD.	815	910	1058	215	430	815	908	1015	1048	1115	1215	1245	115	145	315	415	515
BLACK DOG	820	915	1103	220	432	820	913	1020	1055	1120	1220	1250	120	150	320	420	520
POTTERNE WICK	825	920	1108	225	440	825	918	1025	1100	1125	1225	1255	125	155	325	425	525
POTTERNE	830	925	1113	230	445	830	923	1030	1103	1130	1230	100	130	200	330	430	530
POTTERNE BUTTS	833	928	1116	233	447	833	926	1033	1105	1133	1233	103	133	203	333	433	533
MOUNT PLEASANT	835	930	1118	235	450	835	928	1035	1107	1135	1235	105	135	205	335	435	535
DEVIZES	845	940	1128	245	500	845	938	1045	1115	1145	1245	115	145	215	345	445	545

SUNDAYS

MARKET LAVINGTON	100	130	200	..	700	..	
WEST LAVINGTON	..	..	207	325	..	925	
LITTLETON PANELL	110	135	210	335	710	935	
GREAT CHEVERELL RD.	..	138	215	340	..	940	
BLACK DOG	115	140	220	342	715	942	
POTTERNE WICK	120	143	225	345	720	945	
POTTERNE	123	145	230	348	723	948	
POTTERNE BUTTS	..	147	233	350	..	950	
MOUNT PLEASANT	..	150	235	353	..	953	
DEVIZES	130	200	245	400	730	1000	

MONS., TUES., FRIS. AND SATS.

	SO	SO	SX	SO	SO	SO		SX	SO	SO		SO	SX	SO		
DEVIZES	900	1100	1200	1230	100	200	300	315	430	500	530	630	800	830	845	..
MOUNT PLEASANT	910	1110	1210	1240	110	210	310	325	440	510	540	640	810	840	855	..
POTTERNE BUTTS	912	1112	1212	1242	112	212	312	327	442	512	542	642	812	842	857	..
POTTERNE	915	1115	1215	1245	115	215	315	330	445	515	545	645	815	845	900	..
POTTERNE WICK	920	1120	1220	1250	120	220	320	335	450	520	550	650	820	850	905	..
BLACK DOG	925	1125	1225	1255	125	225	325	340	455	525	555	655	825	855	910	..
GREAT CHEVERELL RD.	930	1130	1230	100	130	230	330	345	500	530	600	700	830	900	915	..
LITTLETON PANELL	935	1135	1235	105	135	235	335	350	505	535	605	705	835	905	920	..
WEST LAVINGTON	940	1140	1240	110	140	240	340	355	510	540	610	710	840	..	925	..
MARKET LAVINGTON	..	1150	1250	120	150	250	350	..	520	550	..	720	850	920	935	..

MONS., TUES., FRIS, AND SATS. (CONT.) — **WEDNESDAYS** — **THURSDAYS**

	SO	SO	SO														
DEVIZES	1015	1030	1100	900	315	430	630	830	900	1100	1200	1230	200	230	300	315	330
MOUNT PLEASANT	1025	1040	1110	910	325	440	640	840	910	1110	1210	1240	210	240	310	325	340
POTTERNE BUTTS	1027	1042	1112	912	327	442	642	842	912	1112	1212	1242	212	242	312	327	342
POTTERNE	1030	1045	1115	915	330	445	645	845	915	1115	1215	1245	215	245	315	330	345
POTTERNE WICK	1035	1050	1120	920	335	450	650	850	920	1120	1220	1250	220	250	320	335	350
BLACK DOG	1040	1055	1125	925	340	455	655	855	925	1125	1225	1255	225	255	325	340	355
GREAT CHEVERELL RD.	1045	1100	1130	930	345	500	700	900	930	1130	1230	100	230	300	330	345	400
LITTLETON PANELL	1050	1105	1135	935	350	505	705	905	935	1135	1235	105	235	305	335	350	405
WEST LAVINGTON	1055	1110	1140	940	355	510	710	910	940	1140	1240	110	240	310	340	355	410
MARKET LAVINGTON	..	1120	1150	..	..	520	720	920	..	1150	1250	120	250	320	350	..	..

THURS. (CONT.) — **SUNDAYS**

DEVIZES	400	500	530	600	130	430	800	830	930	1000	
MOUNT PLEASANT	410	510	540	640	140	..	810	840	940	1010	
POTTERNE BUTTS	412	512	542	642	142	440	812	842	942	1012	
POTTERNE	415	515	545	645	145	..	815	845	945	1015	
POTTERNE WICK	420	520	550	650	150	445	820	850	950	1020	
BLACK DOG	425	525	555	655	155	..	825	855	955	1025	
GREAT CHEVERELL RD.	430	530	600	700	200	450	830	900	1000	1030	
LITTLETON PANELL	435	535	605	705	205	455	835	905	1005	1035	
WEST LAVINGTON	440	540	..	710	210	..	..	910	..	..	
MARKET LAVINGTON	450	550	620	720	..	500	840	920	1010	1040	

SO SATS. ONLY. SX NOT SATS.

857

L&DMS services 410D and 410E from the spring 1931 *Roadway* timetable booklet.

The Horse Era

The earliest recorded transport link from Market Lavington to the outside world was run by the Philpott family of the Green Dragon public house, from around the 1840s. They had a horse-drawn conveyance that is said to have primarily carried goods to a suitable rail head, but on occasion, passenger trips were made to London. This was followed by 'The Hope Coach', run by brothers Enos and Zebedee Price. Their father – James Price – was a carrier in the Fiddington area by the 1850s, and by 1861 (probably earlier), their service was thought to be in operation. In that year's census, Enos, coach proprietor, was living with his mother at 21 Church Street, Market Lavington, while Zebedee was listed as an innkeeper, east of Pewsey. Their service departed from Church Street on Mondays, Wednesdays and Fridays at 10 a.m., bound for Hungerford station via Pewsey, returning the following day at 3.10 p.m., no doubt connecting with the departure and arrival of London trains. This was a relatively lengthy journey on largely unmade roads, and the fares were probably beyond the means of the ordinary working man – 5s on top of the coach and 8s inside it. Local myth says that when a steep hill was encountered, first class passengers rode in the coach, second class passengers walked and third class helped push! How long it survived is unknown, but Enos Price was listed in 1871 as farming at Milton Lilbourne. In later life he returned to live in High Street, Market Lavington. A devout congregational chapel man, he would recount hair-raising tales of driving the coach in all weathers; his riding crop and the footboard from the coach, with the word 'Hope' painted on it, were mounted above his fireplace.

Edwin Potter was born on 6 July 1841, the son of Thomas and Jane. By 1851, Thomas was a butcher and publican at the Angel Inn, Market Lavington, near the corner of Church Street and Parsonage Lane. After Thomas died, his wife took over his professions and in 1861 was still listed as being at the same hostelry, which later became the Volunteer Arms. At that time, Edwin was still at home and was described as a carpenter's apprentice. In 1868, Edwin married his first wife, Sarah Jane Andrews; she sadly died two years later. The next census in 1871 reveals that Edwin and his son Joseph were still living with Jane Potter. Edwin was now described as a 'journeyman carpenter'. However, it is said that by 1872, he replaced his work as a carpenter and

The Volunteer Arms (formerly the Angel Inn) in Church Street, Market Lavington, was the home of Edwin Potter, who was to start a regular horse-drawn bus service from Market Lavington to Devizes. It was also the place where L&DMS founder Fred Sayer initially kept his vehicle. It closed in 1990 and is now a private residence. (Author)

Potter's first omnibus is standing outside Devizes railway station, allegedly in July 1905. Pulled by two horses, it appears to have a fabric-covered top that has got rather ripped in places. Edwin and Ann Potter seem to have some goods on board already for delivery to the Lavingtons. (MLM)

wheelwright with the role of village carrier; he had to give up working with wood as the sawdust aggravated his lungs.

Edwin Potter was by no means the first carrier operating in the Market Lavington and Easterton area. In the mid-1860s, there were three listed as taking goods to and from Devizes and perhaps a few passengers as well – Messrs Axford, Robert Draper (from Easterton) and Dyke, while several others served Potterne and West Lavington en route from Salisbury and other villages scattered around the Plain. However, Edwin started taking goods and produce with his horse and cart from the Market Lavington area to Devizes market or to the railway station in that town. In the reverse direction, he brought supplies from Devizes or further afield into the village for the residents and shopkeepers. In June 1874, Edwin married again; this time his bride was Ann Smith of nearby Easterton.

In the second half of the nineteenth century and for the first twenty-five years or so of the twentieth, most rural communities had their own carrier, doing pretty much the same as Edwin Potter. The carrier's van came in various forms and styles and was usually pulled by one, or more likely two horses. These worked long hours in all weathers and had to be strong, in order to cover the customer requirements in the time available and to ensure that any passengers reached their destination at the advertised time. It was almost always the womenfolk who travelled with the carrier in order to reach the shops or market in the town, as for five and a half days a week the men would be at work.

Edwin, his new wife and six offspring from his two marriages, subsequently moved to Old Bell House in the High Street, between the Green Dragon public house and the Workmen's Hall. The first reference to Potter as an omnibus proprietor is in a directory for 1875; he gravitated to carrying passengers in a one-horse conveyance he purchased from the Draper family, to whom he had been apprenticed. This was replaced in due course by an enclosed vehicle said to carry up to fourteen persons, depending on the amount of goods to be transported, pulled by two horses and painted blue and white with a black top covering. Edwin and Ann gained a reputation for reliability and their horse bus carried local people, as well as goods inside and on the roof, along its route from Easterton and Market Lavington to Devizes via West Lavington Crossroads, Littleton Panell and Potterne. Said to run 'daily', but more likely six days a week, it departed from Market Lavington at 9.30 a.m. and had to be at Devizes post office at 10.35 a.m. in order for the mail to be put on the 11 a.m. train to Bristol. In time, possibly by the 1890s, the horse bus was supplemented by a larger one. This could be pulled by up to four horses, especially useful in heavy snow such as during the periodic blizzards which swept down from Salisbury Plain. On Devizes market day, Thursday, two return trips to town were provided to cope with the demand. The horse buses were run to and from Devizes station for those arriving from or catching trains and for the shipment of inbound and outbound goods and parcels. The Potters also offered conveyances for hire and had a twelve-horse wagon, suitable for carrying heavy goods or undertaking furniture removals.

While Potter served the needs of Easterton and the Lavingtons, John Matthews and then Tom Snook, with his horse-drawn van carrying up to fifteen passengers, provided the link to Devizes from Urchfont – or Erchfont, as it was also spelt at that time. It took forty-five minutes to get there and they both used the White Bear public house in Devizes as the stabling point.

Thus established, Edwin Potter was to continue for many years to be a principal carrier of goods and produce into and out of Easterton, Market Lavington and Potterne as well as providing the only public transport by road to or from Devizes. However, from 1 March 1911, Potter curtailed his horse bus service to run only on Mondays, Thursdays and Saturdays, while the 1913 local directory for Devizes quotes the days as Tuesdays, Thursdays and Saturdays. From 1912 onwards, he probably began to lose passengers to the new motor bus service operated by Bath Electric Tramways Ltd, although early motor vehicles could be unreliable whereas Edwin's horses just needed to be pointed in the right direction. The transport of goods then became the main business once again. Potter was using the yard of the Elm Tree public house in Long Street, Devizes, as his parking place and collection point for goods to be taken to the villages from the town's shopkeepers. By 1914 the Orcheston-based carrier Martha Hall & Sons was running a motor bus on Thursdays through West Lavington and Potterne to Devizes and by about 1915, when the Bath Electric Tramways service is believed to have been taken over by Fred Sayer, Potter may only have been running on Thursdays. After that, he is thought to have continued a passenger service for no more than another year, although he was listed in a 1916 directory as an omnibus and motor car proprietor.

Edwin Potter was also a farmer and was assisted on the farm and in his bus/carrier activities by some of his family, including his son Edwin Albert, born in 1875, who married Mary Ann Pike from West Lavington in spring 1903. Other sons involved with the horse bus were Arthur and Joseph, while Alfred had only been married for two years before he was killed on the Somme in February 1917 while serving in the Royal Warwickshire Regiment. It was unofficially suggested that the proportion of eligible men from the village (population in 1914: 981) who enlisted in the forces was particularly high. Edwin Potter senior died on 6 July 1921, aged seventy-nine, and his wife, Ann, three years later in April 1924. At the time, it was noted that she had made unfailing efforts in terms of supervising the delivery of newspapers and parcels to the village; as a mark of respect, blinds were drawn and shops partially closed along the route of her funeral procession.

After his marriage, Edwin junior set up home in Parsonage Lane in Market Lavington. By 1911 he had three children – Helena May, aged seven, Amy Kathleen, aged five and Edwin John, aged three. Potter descendants still reside locally and the name lives on; a path linking The Spring with The Manor House goes up and down steps to cross two streams. These steps were constructed by Edwin junior in the days after the carrier activities when he worked for Dauntsey's School, which bought The Manor House in 1929. Some older residents still refer to 'Potter's Steps'.

In this delightfully rustic scene, Potter's horse bus is by Cornbury Bridge in Market Lavington, with the mode of passenger access to it clearly visible. The 'Sunday best' clothing of the party with the bus contrasts with that of those engaged in more menial tasks. (MLM)

Outside the Potter residence at Old Bell House in Market Lavington high street, Edwin and the family are seen with the second, larger horse bus, which was a more purpose-built affair. The use of four horses may not have been routine, but was perhaps more for the benefit of the photographer in this posed view. (MLM)

Another view of the later horse bus, which, suitably decorated, is taking part in Trowbridge Carnival. Among the costumes, Edwin sports an imitation Isambard Kingdom Brunel hat. The normal 'Lavington to Devizes' sign writing is partly obscured by the special decorations. (MLM)

One local source has suggested that this charabanc was operated by Potter, although no other evidence of passenger motor vehicle operation has been discovered. It may have been run for a short time in the early 1920s by Edwin Potter junior, who lived in Parsonage Lane in Market Lavington, where it is said the vehicle was kept in a shed. However, here it is thought to be in Weymouth on a private party outing. (MLM)

The Motor Bus Arrives

Like many of the larger urban areas in the British Isles in the later part of the nineteenth century, the city of Bath was to see the introduction of a horse-drawn tramway as well as a number of horse bus routes. However, the formation of Bath Electric Tramways Ltd (BET) on 9 July 1902 is of relevance to our story; it was simply a renaming of the Bath & District Light Railway Co. to effect the provision of an electric tram system in the city and then to operate it under an agreement with the Bath Corporation. Back in 1898, the corporation had received an approach from the British Electric Traction Co. Ltd, but the councillors determined that the tramways should be under their control. They set up an Electric Traction Joint Committee and joined with the promoters of the Bath & District company. Construction work began in November 1902 but it was not until 2 January 1904 that public service commenced on the first routes, including one out to Bathford.

The American general manager of BET, R. D. McCarter, decided in 1904 that he would introduce motor buses to act as feeders to the tramways from the more outlying areas of the city as well as from some of the surrounding towns. The second half of 1905 saw the arrival of six Milnes-Daimler thirty-two-seat open-top double-deck buses with bodywork by Dodson, followed in 1906 by six Bussing double-deck vehicles with thirty-five-seat bodywork by the Bristol Carriage & Wagon Works Co. The chassis were built in Germany and imported by Straker Squire of Bristol, under which name the vehicles were generally described. Bus services were established, including those radiating out from the tram terminus at Bathford Railway Bridge to Frome via Trowbridge, to Chippenham via Box and Corsham and to Melksham via Box, Wormwood, Atworth and Shaw. These were all running by spring 1906 and from 31 May that year, the Melksham service was extended to Devizes via Bowerhill and Seend. The new services proved popular; for example, Trowbridge Urban District Council dealt with an application from BET for licences for nine extra drivers and eleven conductors, as well as receiving a number of complaints of alleged overloading of buses. Devizes Urban District Council granted licences for six buses, nineteen drivers and ten conductors, despite concerns over the council's perceived liability to the public, as licensing authority, should an accident occur.

At the dawn of the motor bus era in the Bath area, Milnes-Daimler FB 05, dating from 1905, stands adjacent to tram No. 28 at the terminus and transfer point near Bathford railway bridge. It was from here that Bath Electric Tramways ran omnibus services to several towns in Wiltshire and to Frome in Somerset, connecting with trams from the city centre, as suggested by the sign on the lamp column that states, 'Alight here for motor omnibuses.' (J. Batten Collection)

Devizes Chamber of Commerce had once asked the Great Western Railway to run road motor services from villages near the military camps on Salisbury Plain into the town, but the GWR declined. However, by September 1906, Devizes Council, egged on by the mayor's enthusiasm, had opened negotiations with BET to ascertain whether the company would consider providing services from Potterne, the Lavingtons, Tilshead, Upavon and Rushall into Devizes. The company agreed in principle if three buses could be garaged in Devizes during a trial period of operation. Mr W. Dickenson, a carrier on the canal and the lessee of Devizes Wharf, said he would erect a shed on his premises which BET could use rent-free. BET were asked to consider two circular routes to be operated experimentally for six weeks – one covering Potterne, Littleton Panell, Market Lavington, Urchfont and Stert and a more ambitious one via West Lavington, Tilshead, Shrewton, Amesbury, 'The Bournes' and Upavon. BET were not particularly interested in the latter but suggested a route from Devizes to Calne instead.

A test run of their two preferred routes was carried out by BET with a bus on 5 October 1906. This was driven by foreman engineer J. S. Warwick, with McCarter and William Eversley Hardy (McCarter's deputy) on board. Possibly sensing a jolly good day out in the offing, the Mayor of Bath and Alderman Taylor, Chairman of the Tramways Committee, went along for the ride. On arrival at Devizes they were joined by local civic dignitaries and representatives from the Chamber of Commerce. In the morning they went round the proposed Market Lavington route, during which there was a seven-minute break at Potterne to allow the bus engine to cool down after ascending the steep hill. The party then adjourned to the Castle Hotel in Devizes for lunch and speeches. Alderman Taylor said that BET would not make much money initially 'but it did not matter as the shareholders were rich men who did not seek large dividends' (laughter). In the afternoon, the bus continued to Calne, raising curiosity in the villages it passed through. After another civic welcome party, the bus went on to Chippenham. At the end of the day, McCarter was non-committal but immediately decided against the Calne–Chippenham section. The party returned to the Castle Hotel for tea, where the BET officers were pressed for their opinion. The story was that the bus garage shed to be built in Devizes should cost no more than £12, but BET thought that £120 would have to be spent to make it robust enough for their requirements. The outcome of the day was that BET pledged to start just the Market Lavington circular service for an initial three-week trial period, with four journeys from late November 1906, when more new buses had been delivered.

However, no doubt to municipal frustration and disappointment, BET abandoned their plans in December 1906, due, it was said, to strong objections from people in Devizes and the villages. BET's Wiltshire activities continued much as before. Operating in a bronze green livery from the garage at Kensington in Bath, the Straker Squire vehicles were used on the Bathford-based services, including the one to Devizes. Although the latter seems to have operated daily at least until autumn 1907, it became seasonal from then onwards, generally from April or May to a date in October. Days of operation then varied, but most consistent were Thursdays and Saturdays, with three or four round trips and two on Sundays. In the high summers of 1907–9, Tuesdays also

In 1906 Bath Electric Tramways purchased six Bussing double deck vehicles with thirty-five-seat bodywork by the Bristol Carriage & Wagon Works. More often known as a Straker Squire, after the name of the importing agent, here is FB 012 labelled for the service to Melksham and Devizes – the first motor bus service to the latter town. Vehicle registrations issued by Bath County Borough Council at this time unusually contained a zero before the number, to denote a 'heavy' vehicle. (J. Batten Collection)

featured. By 1908, in which year, on 30 June, McCarter departed and was replaced by a promoted Hardy, the single fare from Bathford to Devizes had risen to 1s 5d, an increment of 1d over the previous year. BET also used their buses for private hire and pleasure trips from Bath to take the many visitors to places such as Stonehenge, Cheddar, Portishead and Clevedon.

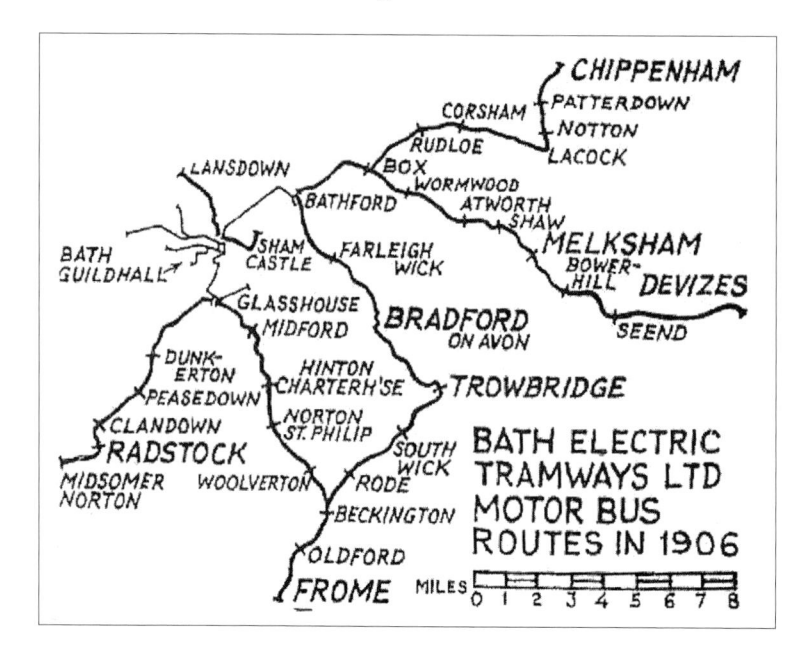

Edwin Potter's decision to reduce his horse bus service in March 1911, perhaps as a result of losing the contract to carry the mail, had not gone down too well with Devizes Chamber of Commerce, who feared that people in the Lavingtons might be tempted to go shopping in towns that could be reached direct by rail, rather than in Devizes. By summer 1911, Potter was being pressured from certain quarters to restore the six days per week service, responding that he would not even consider it – 'I am not keen on the thing at all and it would take very little to upset the existing three days a week.' When approached, BET chanced their luck by suggesting that they would require a £40 per annum revenue guarantee to run a service from the Lavingtons. However, local cash donations and pledges raised only £12 for the cause.

Somebody signing himself 'A Wheel within a Wheel', from Market Lavington, wrote to the *Wiltshire Gazette*, saying 'I congratulate Mr Potter for curtailing his journeys to Devizes and the sooner he discontinues them altogether, the better for him and for Lavington'. He then went on to assert that everything for local needs could be purchased in Market Lavington itself. 'I say – let us stay at home, we are content and let Devizes do the same. I fail to see anything in Devizes to take me there, either by Potter's bus or by rail.' However, the waters of local public opinion were about to close over this person's head as support for a direct bus service to Devizes was more encouraging than expected. There was desire for it from 'all classes', including from farmers who would not need to use their own conveyances.

The president of Devizes Chamber of Commerce, Charles Parsons, went with Mr W. Young of West Lavington to see Hardy, in Bath, to campaign again for a service; large petitions of support had come from Market Lavington and Potterne. They got the impression that Hardy was almost ready to send a bus at once and on asking Young about garage accommodation in Market Lavington, he was told that 'that would be an easy matter'. In December, BET announced that the service would start the following spring, when a 'new type of vehicle had been constructed for it', with two round trips per day. On 24 April 1912 the 'new' bus took one hour and twenty minutes to come from Bath to Devizes in order to be tested on the Market Lavington route. It may have been FB 011, originally one of the Straker Squire double deckers of 1906, which had been fitted by BET with a modified single-deck Dodson body, which had been removed from one of the original Milnes-Daimler vehicles, turned back to front and converted to single-deck form. It was quoted as being of 32 hp, had twenty-seven seats and a glass-panelled entrance door to the side of the driver. Its sides were open but these were to be glassed-in before the winter. As it passed through Potterne, a resident excitedly waved a Union Flag, while, during a thirty-minute break outside the Green Dragon pub in Market Lavington, many people came to stare at this modern wonder. BET officials inspected a building at the rear of the pub to see if it was suitable to use as a bus garage, but the roof was found to be too low. A drawing of the vehicle was printed in the *Wiltshire Gazette* on 16 May with details of the proposed timetable – journeys would leave Market Lavington at 10 a.m., 2 p.m. and 5.30 p.m., returning from Devizes at 12 noon, 3 p.m. and 6.30 p.m. There would be no service on Wednesdays, when the bus would be made available for private hire and perhaps 'only an occasional trip on Sundays', when there might be an odd journey via Easterton and Urchfont instead of Potterne.

BET facilitated their satellite operation by locating two vehicles and drivers at Market Lavington, where the yard of the King's Arms public house was said to have been initially used as a base. The service to Devizes via West Lavington Crossroads, Littleton Panell and Potterne started on 1 June 1912. The timetable showed three journeys each way except for Wednesdays, with an extra one on Saturdays. On Sundays, the journey at 3 p.m. from Devizes, returning from Market Lavington at 7.20 p.m., did indeed run via Urchfont and Easterton. The single fare from Market Lavington to Devizes was 6d and the journey time was forty minutes for the 5-mile distance, with the 12 mph maximum speed allowed at that time. From 20 July 1912, an additional trip at 8 p.m. on Saturdays from Devizes to Potterne and back was provided, while from 1 November there was one round trip less on Mondays, Tuesdays and Fridays. There appeared in the July 1913 BET timetable booklet an additional three journeys each way from Market Lavington to Devizes on Thursdays and Saturdays via Easterton and Urchfont, requiring the use of a second bus, but this was seemingly transient as there was no reference to them in the September 1913 edition.

At least three of the Straker Squire vehicles were subsequently photographed in Market Lavington, two of them after being converted to single-deckers. FB 011, already mentioned, had received its modified body in March 1912 and FB 08 had a twenty-seven-seat body (possibly also by Dodson, from one of the early double-deck vehicles) modified and fitted by BET in June 1913. However, while views of Straker Squire FB 013

We now meet the Sayer family, sitting regally at the front of Bath Electric Tramways Straker Squire FB 011. Fred of course, is the driver, next to him is his wife Mabel with son Fred junior, and then comes Fred's mother, Mary Sare. (L. Tancock Collection)

at Market Lavington show it in double-deck form, by 1913 it was fitted with a charabanc body removed from a Commer WP2 registered FB 028 or 029. After the outbreak of the First World War, by October 1914 the chassis of BET Straker Squires FB 08–012 were recorded as requisitioned by the War Office for potential use as military transport, along with the chassis of ten out of the thirteen Commer vehicles (for which £5,458 was paid), including charabancs used on excursions from Bath. Motor bus services in Bath and the tramway feeder services were eventually reduced or suspended. For the summers of 1913 and 1914, the one from Bathford to Devizes only ran on Sundays; it did not reappear as such in subsequent years. Exactly which BET vehicles operated on the Market Lavington service after autumn 1914 is not determined.

BET advertised a 'charabanc' excursion to run on 30 August 1914, leaving Market Lavington at 2 p.m. via Potterne and Devizes to Durrington Camp, returning at 7 p.m. This was where the 4th Battalion of the Wilts Regiment was located and the trip may have been to allow relatives of servicemen to visit them, perhaps before potentially being sent off overseas. The fare was 3s 6d, with seats bookable with the driver of the Lavington bus.

The arrival of BET in Market Lavington sets the scene for the introduction of one of the principal characters in this story – Frederick Herbert Sayer. He was born in Bath in the summer of 1880, the son of Frederick Sare and the former Mary Emily Ballin. His parents always spelt their name Sare – it was probably originally Sayre – but in later life Fred used the Sayer spelling. The family had a linen draper's shop in Kingsmead Square

Parked on the corner of the marketplace in Market Lavington, Fred waits in summer 1912 for the local commercial photographer to capture Bath Electric Tramways Straker Squire FB 011 after conversion to a single-deck vehicle for the new service thence to Devizes. Junior members of the Baker family also appear. The reverse of the postcard is inscribed, 'This is our new motor bus that runs every day from Lavington to Devizes, so you see we are getting more like London here.' (MLM)

Another Bath Electric Tramways Straker Squire single-deck conversion used at Market Lavington was FB 08, here at the junction of High Street, Church Street, Parsonage Lane and White Street. In the background is the King's Arms public house, the yard of which was said to have been used by BET for parking their vehicles. (MLM)

in Bath but later became furriers at 16 Union Street. It is thought that Fred's father died in 1892, and a few years later Fred became a railway porter at King's Norton in Worcestershire. He became engaged to Mabel Weston, of a similar age, whose family also came from Bath; they married at King's Norton towards the end of 1900. By spring 1911, Fred and Mabel were living at Brewery Lane in Nailsworth, Gloucestershire, with their son, born in early 1906 and also named, imaginatively, Frederick Herbert. Fred was described as a tram, car and bus driver and as a motor mechanic.

It is thought that Fred Sayer arrived in Market Lavington when the BET service started and he may well have worked for that firm previously; his son had been born in the Bath district. The earliest available Market Lavington register of electors giving his name is that for 1915, when he was living at The Terrace, off Northbrook, just beyond the Market Place. Despite the exigencies of war, the motor bus service between Market Lavington and Devizes (marketplace) was still running and in a local directory for 1915 Fred is listed as 'Bath Motor Bus Local Manager', which probably meant he was lead driver, mechanic and general factotum. His later vehicle engineering and bus-building activities probably confirmed his skill and resourcefulness. However, it appears that by autumn 1915, he became a motor bus proprietor. As the Market Lavington–Devizes service was not listed in the BET timetable booklet of May 1915 onwards, this event could have occurred earlier. Who approached whom is uncertain, but BET seem to have decided that in the wartime circumstances they needed to concentrate their limited resources on operations in Bath itself and on one or two more remunerative country services such as that to Frome. Therefore, the Market Lavington to Devizes service passed to Fred Sayer on his own account, perhaps initially under some form of 'arrangement', although documentary confirmation of the circumstances is lacking. However, the Bath-based company was to maintain links with Fred's operations throughout this story.

An advertisement in the local press in the first week of November 1915 announced that two new services were about to start, without mentioning the name of the operator, but on balance this was felt likely to be Sayer. A charabanc would run on Tuesdays to Salisbury for the market, leaving Market Lavington at 9 a.m. to travel via Easterton, Urchfont, Devizes, Potterne and West Lavington, arriving Salisbury at 10.30 a.m. and returning from there at 3.30 p.m. The fare was 3*s* 6*d* return from the Lavingtons and 4*s* from Devizes. Every Wednesday a bus or charabanc would run to Bath from Market Lavington (9 a.m.) via Potterne, Devizes, Seend, Bowerhill, Melksham, Shaw, Atworth, Wormwood, Box and Bathford. The bus returned at 5 p.m., the journey taking two hours and ten minutes. The fare for the full journey was 2*s* single, 3*s* 6*d* return. In Bath, it was stated that the 'car will be garaged at the Bath Tramways depot, Walcot Street and passengers may have their parcels sent there, addressed: Devizes bus'. This service featured in the post-war Bath Tramways timetable books, so it may also have been run by Sayer under some form of arrangement with that company. In fact, until the middle of 1921, the page for the Market Lavington services was headed 'Bath Electric Tramways'; after that, by which time Sayer had expanded the Bath service, it just stated 'Motor Services'. Conversely, the Salisbury excursion seems not to have been perpetuated in the longer term, as it was not featured in the BET timetable booklets and was not mentioned in a newspaper advertisement listing Sayer's operations in January 1920.

Fred Sayer again with Straker Squire FB 08, surrounded by soldiers from the 4th Wiltshire Territorial Army, who were apparently being taken to their camp in 1914, shortly before the vehicle was requisitioned by the War Department. (MLM)

Bath Electric Tramways Straker Squire FB 013 was captured on film while still in double-deck form, with the Market Lavington Prize Silver Band, although it is recorded as having been re-bodied as a charabanc before being scrapped in July 1913. It stands outside the Volunteer Arms, where William Trotter was then the landlord and also a firewood dealer. Trotter's daughter would eventually marry Fred Sayer junior. (MLM)

In 1915 an 'Our Day' sale was held in Market Lavington marketplace to raise money for the Red Cross. Of relevance to our story is the imposing house in the background, once occupied by the local doctor, with Mr Oatley's premises to its left. In the 1920s, these buildings were partly demolished to make way for parking L&DMS buses, which will be seen later. (MLM)

From at least 1915 until 1932, the Sayer family lived at 'Ivydene', on The Terrace in Market Lavington. This is the house on the right behind the lady, and it was also to be the office and headquarters of Lavington & Devizes Motor Services until 1938. A garage and workshop stood behind it. In what is probably an Edwardian-era photograph, the road known as Northbrook drops down on the left. (MLM)

Post-War Recovery

Sayer's first vehicles in 1915–17 are not recorded – perhaps he had some on hire from BET under an agreement for taking over the Market Lavington service, assuming they could spare them. However, in September 1918 he acquired an Overland charabanc (AM 4980) from E. W. Grant of Winterbourne Stoke and in April 1919 obtained FB 028, a Commer WP2 charabanc from the War Department, which had been requisitioned from BET in 1914. With better availability of petrol, such vehicles could once again be used for pleasure trips, such as to coastal resorts, which the populace were eager to indulge in as a means of escaping memories of the hardships and the aftermath of war. However, with a folding canvas hood in place in poor weather, they could perhaps be used on bus services. In 1920, Sayer obtained a Commer RC-type chassis and fitted it with a thirty-two-seat front-entrance saloon bus body, constructed partly by Dodson and partly by BET, purchased from the latter and then modified and registered HR 655. Pre-war, this body was of a twenty-seven-seat rear entrance type, on one of BET's Commer WP1 buses, either FB 032 or 033. Following this, there arrived in August 1920 a canvas-roofed Crossley carrier's van (HR 2587), which could accommodate fourteen passengers. Interestingly, Sayer adopted a similar dark bronze green livery to that of BET.

As well as the bus activities, Sayer was listed in 1920 as a motor car proprietor and had two goods vehicles for hire. During the 1920s it seems that some vehicles were used either in charabanc or lorry form as required, involving a degree of body-changing. By March 1920, he had adopted the trading name of Lavington & Devizes Motor Services (L&DMS), with a sub-title of Green Charabancs, for his coaching activities. Advertising stated:

> Torpedo charabancs and buses seating twenty six to thirty for hire. Parties of twenty to two hundred catered for. Visit Cheddar and see the wonders of your own country. Fast and luxurious travelling at low cost. Frequent trips will be run in the Season to places of interest.

Bath Tramways also used the word 'Torpedo' to describe their charabancs. L&DMS advertising advised that on Easter Monday 5 April 1920, 'the usual bus service will run

The first recorded L&DMS single-deck bus (as opposed to a charabanc) was this Commer-registered HR655 from around 1919/20. On a chassis returned from war service was mounted a body obtained from Bath Electric Tramways and modified, containing part of one made by Dodson, which pre-war had been BET's rear-entrance single-deck vehicle FB 032 or 033. Note the steep steps at the entrance, the tailboard at the rear for carrying goods and the ladder hanging on the side for roof access for further goods stowage. The driver is Charlie Sheppard, and the conductor is Harry Cooper. (MLM)

to Bath'. This was shown as leaving Devizes at 9.30 a.m., 1.30 p.m. and 5.30 p.m. and leaving Bathford tram terminus at 11.25 a.m., 3.25 p.m. and 7.25 p.m. Some mystery surrounds this as Sayer seems to have reactivated the former BET tramway feeder service, perhaps on a one-off basis. Also on Easter Monday, a charabanc excursion was run to Weston-super-Mare, leaving Market Lavington at 9 a.m., with a fare of 11s 6d – a real treat for those able to afford it.

Sayer's abode at The Terrace was called Ivydene; part of the house was used as an office, where he could sometimes be found residing in a large leather swivelling chair. At the rear was a building used as a bus garage and workshop as well as a yard area, accessed from the north-east corner of the marketplace.

The motor bus and general goods haulage activities of Bath Electric Tramways Ltd were separated from the tramway operations on 30 July 1920, with the formation and registration of an associated company called Bath Tramways Motor Co. Ltd (BTMC). High operating costs and reduced revenue during the war and afterwards meant that BET had not paid shareholder dividends for some time, which made it difficult to

For comparative purposes, this image shows how the body of the L&DMS vehicle in the previous photograph appeared when previously mounted on a 1913 Bath Electric Tramways Commer. Part of it had come from one of the original Dodson bodies on the 1905 Milnes-Daimler double-deckers, with additions by BET's own workshop. (J. Batten Collection)

Not the clearest of images but interesting as it contains a fine line-up of most of the Commer charabancs put on the road by Fred Sayer in 1921, all numbered and loaded for a major private hire booking for a firm's outing in somewhat damp conditions. Male headgear was *de rigeur*. The Commer chassis were reconditioned after military use, with some dating back to 1913. The nearest one is AM 9059, a Commer WP1 with twenty-eight seats, registered in January 1921. (L. Tancock Collection)

raise capital to renew and expand the bus fleet. BTMC also took over the foundry at the Walcot Street tram depot, which had been quite profitable in terms of work undertaken. Under an agreement, BTMC paid BET £19,935 in cash and £20,000 in share acquisitions. BET's and BTMC's registered office was at Balfour House, 119–125 Finsbury Pavement, London EC2.

From 1 November 1920, Sayer added a Monday trip to Bath, to supplement the Wednesday one. There was also a Saturday round trip from Market Lavington to Devizes and Bath, leaving at 2.00 p.m. and returning at 9.30 p.m. The through fare was increased to 2s 9d single, 5s return. A journey from Bath to Devizes on Thursdays, leaving at 9.45 a.m. and returning initially at 4.30 p.m., was worked by a BTMC vehicle. There was competition for Sayer in terms of custom for a trip from Devizes to Bath. On 22 September 1920, Edwin and Charles Sudweeks of the Bear Hotel Garage, Devizes, started two trips on Wednesdays with their Napier charabanc. They will reappear later in this story.

A L&DMS excursion was advertised for 8 June 1921 for a trip to Portsmouth to witness the launch of the hull of the new HMS *Effingham*, a Royal Navy heavy cruiser, although it was not finally commissioned until 1925.

Despite the apparent consensus between the two operators, it seems that BTMC were concerned about Sayer's potential future activities. It was decided in September 1921 that William Hardy should meet with Sayer in terms of an agreement of some sort being reached in order to safeguard BTMC interests in the Market Lavington area. At the same time, BTMC was also proposing a territorial agreement with the National Omnibus & Transport Co. Ltd, which was then expanding in the West

Another rugged Commer charabanc, a thirty-two-seat WP1 model with a 1913 chassis, was AM 9699, registered in March 1921. The occasion was a day trip to Trowbridge, for a political rally, by the West Lavington branch of the Workers' Union, photographed near Dauntsey's school. (R. Grimley Collection)

Opposite: AM 9698 was a twenty-eight-seat charabanc on a Commer RC chassis, also first registered in January 1921. This view is thought to date from one or two years later; the driver was Percy Notton. Joe Gye and Charles Ross have alighted to stretch their legs during a break in Salisbury. (MLM)

Country, having originated with operations in London and Essex. This company and one of its subsequent offspring were to be active in west Wiltshire for around fifty years. Some have advanced the theory that Sayer was a 'front' for BTMC, being covertly supported by the larger concern in a sensitive boundary zone, or, at least, his expansionist activities were tolerated in order to stop National O&T and Wilts & Dorset Motor Services from consolidating their networks in the Devizes area. However, no documentary proof has yet been uncovered.

Boundaries and Opportunities

After the First World War, bus operators who in due course would become major and long-lived players were striving to establish a framework of inter-urban services in an attempt to in-fill large tracts of the West Country into their aspired territories, including in rural areas where small operators or village carriers were rapidly embracing the motor vehicle. As well as having to face local competition, they were constrained by the difficulty of not being able to obtain sufficient vehicles, or in some cases by a lack of capital. In the general area of interest to this account, these principal operators were the aforementioned Bath Tramways Motor Co. Ltd, the Bristol Tramways & Carriage Co. Ltd, the National Omnibus & Transport Co. Ltd and Wilts & Dorset Motor Services Ltd. The development of services, boundaries and the inter-relationship between them was complex and is largely outside the scope of this story and well-chronicled elsewhere.

In August 1921, National O&T made its first incursion into Wiltshire by opening a base at Trowbridge and established services from there to Chippenham, Frome, Westbury and Bradford on Avon. However, that summer, although their services were still well-separated, National and Wilts & Dorset drew up an area agreement to delineate their aspirations, with a boundary line passing through Warminster, Devizes and Marlborough. In early September 1921, a service was commenced by National from Trowbridge to Devizes via Hilperton, Semington and Seend, with four round trips on weekdays and three on Sundays. This was numbered 5 in March 1922, renumbered 60 in September of that year and then 238 in 1930. Frustratingly, as soon as the agreement was ratified, Bristol Tramways captured Swindon and put out a daily service 71 in January 1922 from there to Devizes via Avebury and Bishops Cannings, as well as services in other areas, which effectively stopped National's and Wilts & Dorset's plans in their tracks. Wilts & Dorset was not at that time in a strong position and had not yet reached Devizes, the area to the south and east of which was in the hands of various small bus operators and carriers, including of course Lavington & Devizes Motor Services. The stage was set for Fred Sayer to gain a shrewd advantage, although Market Lavington was theoretically on the Wilts & Dorset side of the new boundary with National O&T. Within two years, his business was to expand at an almost meteoric rate, capitalising on the desire of local people to undertake both essential and leisure travel, quite different to before the war, when many folk hardly ever left their home villages.

Making the most of the difficulty for National and Wilts & Dorset in crossing the boundary in breach of the area agreement, therefore constraining their abilities to effectively retaliate, Sayer took the opportunity to expand his bus activities by providing services from one company's territory into that of the other. Whether this was with, or without, the support of BTMC is unknown. From the week commencing Sunday 12 June 1921, a number of service enhancements were introduced. Sayer's journeys on the Market Lavington to Bath service were increased to operate daily except Thursdays. There was one return journey on Mondays, Tuesdays, Wednesdays, Fridays and Saturdays which gave a long stay in Bath, and two on Sundays. BTMC had introduced two Devizes to Melksham round trips, worked in the layover time of their Thursday Bath to Devizes market day service and also provided a Sunday round trip between those towns. Sayer initiated a round trip from Market Lavington to Chippenham on Fridays for the market via Devizes, Rowde, Bromham, Sandy Lane and Derry Hill. This departed at 9 a.m. and returned at 3 p.m. There was also a new

Early L&DMS charabancs were somewhat uncomfortable and fairly rudimentary in design, with spoked wheels and thin solid tyres. Likely to be a Commer, it had seven separate doors on the nearside and two wooden running boards due to the height off the ground, which must have been a challenge for elderly or less mobile members of the party. After a journey along the dusty roads of Salisbury Plain, the wheels had a coating of chalk dust; hopefully not too much found its way on to the party's best clothes. (L. Tancock Collection)

Tuesday, Thursday and Saturday service from Market Lavington to Trowbridge via West Lavington Crossroads, Little Cheverell, Erlestoke, Tinhead, Edington, Bratton, Steeple Ashton and Hilperton. On Thursdays, a bus worked back from Trowbridge at 10.15 a.m. to Erlestoke and then northwards through Great Cheverell and Potterne to Devizes, returning at 3.30 p.m. This was performed between the trips to Trowbridge from and back to Market Lavington. Then, from 31 August, Sayer introduced a second service from Market Lavington to Bath, on Wednesdays, departing at 8.30 a.m. and returning at 6 p.m. This was routed via West Lavington Crossroads, Little Cheverell, Erlestoke, Tinhead, Edington, Bratton, Steeple Ashton, Keevil and Semington to Melksham, where it joined the other service to Bath. The Market Lavington to Devizes 'local' service had an improved Thursday timetable, a new Wednesday afternoon journey was introduced from Market Lavington to Bath via Devizes at 1.30 p.m., returning at 9.30 p.m. (this was seemingly unsuccessful and did not endure) and a Saturday afternoon Bath to Devizes round trip was added.

Introduced shortly afterwards, probably in autumn 1921, was another service linking Market Lavington and Devizes, but by way of Easterton, Urchfont, Chirton, Marden, Woodborough, Alton Barnes, All Cannings, Allington and Horton – a truly rural meander. There was one round trip the whole way on Tuesdays, Thursdays and Saturdays and a Saturday evening facility from Woodborough to Devizes aimed at those seeking late shopping or evening entertainment. Finally for 1921, some Wednesday journeys on the 'local' service were added by November, making it a daily operation. By February 1922, there was a round trip from Market Lavington to Trowbridge on Mondays, Wednesdays and Fridays, with additional journeys on Saturday afternoons and evenings. However, the Woodborough service was enlarged from 24 April 1922 by being amended to start at Pewsey to run to Devizes on Mondays to Saturdays via Manningford Bruce, Woodbridge Inn, North Newnton, Hilcot and Bottlesford to Woodborough, then as previously. Three trips each way were provided, with an extra one back from Devizes on Saturdays at 9.00 p.m., which returned from Pewsey to Market Lavington. The 6.30 p.m. trip from Pewsey was routed back to Devizes through Urchfont and Market Lavington. Thus, another part of Wiltshire, in Wilts & Dorset's chosen territory, was added to the L&DMS operating area, although other small firms were also active.

As already mentioned, the early 1920s saw an increase in demand for leisure travel, with a multitude of operators large and small equipping themselves with charabancs which could be run open-topped in fine weather or with a folding canvas hood in place for when it rained or was generally inclement. The seats were arranged in rows right across the vehicle, with a separate door to each row. At that time, they had large brass headlamps lit by acetylene, but were later modified to run electrically from a battery. Until around 1927/8, L&D vehicles had solid tyres. Sunday trips to coastal resorts were especially popular and could be the social event of the year for many village people, such as for children from the Sunday School and their families. These excursions were either on a publically advertised basis or were chartered privately by bespoke groups, being keenly anticipated in advance and talked about long afterwards. The influx of men returning from the forces meant there was a good supply of trained drivers and

Seemingly carrying a few more people than the fourteen seats nominally provided, this looks like one of the Crossleys on a chassis likely previously used for war transport purposes. If the driver is the person in uniform standing at the front, he looks very youthful. (MLM)

those with mechanical skills. There was also a significant number of surplus vehicles, either complete or in chassis form, that could form the basis of a bus or charabanc. These could be bought from war surplus disposal depots, such as at Slough in Berkshire. Commer, Crossley and AEC had been popular makes of vehicle with War Department motor transport officers and large quantities were available at reasonable prices. For an operator with engineering capabilities and skills, or for one able to afford for new bodywork to be constructed, these offered a cost-effective opportunity for meeting demand and business expansion.

Fred Sayer would have been familiar with the products of the Commer Car Co. from his time with Bath Electric Tramways and in 1921/22 he put at least ten on the road, of either the WP1 or the RC model. These were supplemented by six Crossley X-types, which had been particularly popular with the RAF. The chassis were probably all second-hand, some ex-War Department and some dating back to 1913; most were given (or had) charabanc-style bodies, the Crossleys seating fourteen and the Commers mainly twenty-eight or thirty-two. However, two or three of them carried saloon bodywork suitable for use as service buses. These were quite high off the ground and most of the early buses were fitted with a carrier on the back or on the roof for carrying parcels and for taking goods to market, such as crates of poultry. Once ready for the road, they were given contemporary Wiltshire registration numbers. Other chassis may have been acquired at the same time and held in reserve for future use. Also licensed, in May 1922, was HR

A few of the early L&DMS vehicles were fitted with enclosed bodies, which were more suitable for bus work and also more appropriate for outings on wet days. This could be one of the Commers from 1921/2, but unfortunately we cannot see the front end or registration number. There is no glass in the side windows, just a rolled-up canvas that could be lowered. The charabanc to the rear has its simple canvas covering in place and the bonnet side panel open, hopefully for engine-cooling purposes rather than because of a disappointing terminal failure. (MLM)

6694, a former War Department Commer lorry of 1917 vintage, while in February 1922 a 1918 Crossley 25 hp car had been registered to Mabel Sayer as HR 6083.

The rapid expansion of his operations and fleet had no doubt put Fred Sayer under some financial pressure, with a need for more capital. This was alleviated by bringing in outside investors under the constitution of a formal limited liability company arrangement. The future involvement of these outsiders may have surfaced some time in advance, as in May 1922 BTMC were still keen to acquire an interest in Sayer's services and as recent negotiations had not been fruitful (Sayer's proposed terms were not considered acceptable), they decided to make a fresh approach to 'the new owners'. If this occurred, it was without success. In the changing socio-economic circumstances, Sayer's activities were perhaps now viewed as potentially threatening.

Lavington and Devizes Motor Services, Ltd.

Market Lavington, Devizes, and Trowbridge.

	Daily	Daily	Mkt.days only	Saturdays	Saturdays	Daily	Daily	Thurs. Daily	Daily	Sats.	Sats.	Sundays	Sundays
	a.m.	a.m.	a.m.	a.m.	p.m.	p.m.	p.m.	p.m.	p.m.	p.m.	p.m.	p.m.	p.m.
M. LAVINGTON d.	9 0	a9..55	10 30	12 30	...	2 0	...	...	5 10	7 30	...	1 30	5 30
Devizes	...	...	...	...	...	...	*4 30	3 30	...	...	8 30	...	...
Potterne	...	...	...	...	...	...	*4 38	3 45	...	...	8 45	...	...
Littleton Panell	9 5	a10...0	10 35	12 35	...	2 5	...	...	5 15	7 35	...	1 35	5 35
Great Cheverell	9 10	a10...5	10 40	12 40	...	2 10	*4 50	4 10	5 20	7 40	9 0	1 40	5 40
Erlestoke	9 15	a10..10	10 45	12 45	...	2 15	...	4 15	5 25	7 45	...	1 45	5 45
Tinhead	9 25	a10..20	10 55	12 55	...	2 25	...	4 25	5 35	7 55	...	1 55	5 55
Edington	9 30	a10..25	11 0	1 0	...	2 30	...	4 30	5 40	8 0	...	2 0	6 0
Bratton	9 35	a10..30	11 5	1 5	...	2 35	...	4 35	5 45	8 5	...	2 5	6 5
Steeple Ashton	9 45	10 40	11 15	1 15	2 0	2 45	3 35	4 45	5 55	8 15	...	2 15	6 15
Hilperton	9 55?	10 50	11 25	1 25	2 15	2 55	3 45	4 55	6 5	8 25	...	2 25	6 25
TROWBRIDGE a.	10 0	11 0	11 30	1 30	2 20	3 0	3 50	5 0	6 10	8 30	...	2 30	6 30

	Daily	Daily	Daily	Sats.	Daily	Mkt.days only	Daily	Sats.	Thurs. & Sats.	Daily	Sats.	Sundays	Sundays
	a.m.	a.m.	p.m.	p.m.	p.m.	p.m.	p.m.	p.m.	p.m.	p.m.	p.m.	p.m.	p.m.
TROWBRIDGE d.	...	10 15	12 30	1 40	3 10	3 30	4 0	5 30	6* 0	9 0	10 45	3 0	9 0
Hilperton	...	10 20	12 40	1 50	3 20	3 35	4 5	5 35	6 5	9 5	10 50	3 5	9 5
Steeple Ashton	...	10 30	12 45	2 0	3 30	3 45	4 15	5 45	6 15	9 15	11 0	3 15	9 15
Bratton	...	10a40	12 55	...	...	3 55	4 25	...	6 25	9 25	11 10	3 25	9 25
Edington	...	10a45	1 0	...	...	4 0	4 30	...	6 30	9 30	11 15	3 30	9 30
Tinhead	...	10a50	1 5	...	...	4 5	4 35	...	6 35	9 35	11 20	3 35	9 35
Erlestoke	...	11a 0	1 15	...	...	4 15	4 45	...	6 45	9 45	11 30	3 45	9 45
Great Cheverell	*8 25	11a15	1 20	...	...	4 20	4 50	5 30	6 50	9 50	11 35	3 50	9 50
Littleton Panell	...	...	1 25	...	...	4 25	4 55	...	6 55.	9 55	11 40	3 55	9 55
Potterne	*8 37	11a30	...	...	...	...	...	5 45	...	...	...	...	...
Devizes	*8 45	11a45	...	...	...	...	...	6 0	...	...	...	...	...
M. LAVINGTON a.	...	...	1 30	...	...	4 30	5 0	...	7 0	10 0	11 45	4 0	10 0

a—Thursdays only. *—Runs 30 minutes later on Saturdays.

*—This trip only runs during the Devizes Secondary School term.

FARE TABLE.

										To and From	To and From	To and From
										Trowbridge	Lav'n	Devizes
TROWBRIDGE										...	2s. 6d.	3s. 0d.
2d.	Hilperton									3d.	2s. 3d.	2s. 6d.
4d.	3d.	Stoney Gutter								7d.	2s. 0d.	2s. 6d.
6d.	4d.	3d.	Steeple Ashton							10d.	1s. 9d.	2s. 0d.
9d.	7d.	5d.	3d.	Bratton						1s. 3d.	1s. 6d.	2s. 0d.
10d.	8d.	6d.	5d.	2d.	Edington					1s. 3d.	1s. 4d.	1s. 9d.
10d.	9d.	7d	6d.	3d.	2d.	Tinhead				1s. 3d.	1s. 2d.	1s. 8d.
1s. 0d.	10d.	9d	8d.	5d.	4d.	3d.	Erlestoke			1s. 6d.	10d.	1s. 6d.
1s. 3d.	1s. 1d.	1s. 0d.	10d.	8d.	6d.	5d.	3d.	Great Cheverell		2s. 0d.	7d.	1s. 0d.
1s. 4d.	1s. 2d.	1s. 1d.	11d.	9d.	8d.	6d.	4d.	3d.	Littleton Panell	2s. 3d.	...	1s. 0d.
1s. 6d.	1s. 4d.	1s. 2d.	1s. 0d.	9d.	8d.	6d.	4d.	2d.	Lavington	2s. 6d.	...	1s. 0d.
1s. 9d.	1s 7d.	1s. 5d.	1s. 3d.	1s. 0d.	10d.	9d.	7d.	4d.	6d. Potterne	2s. 6d.	1s. 0d.	6d.
2s. 0d.	1s. 10d.	1s. 8d.	1s. 4d.	1s. 3d.	1s. 2d.	1s. 0d.	1s. 0d.	6d.	6d. 4d. DEVIZES	3s. 0d.	1s. 0d.	...

Market Lavington,
Wilts,
November, 1932.

Woodward, Printer, Devizes.

A timetable from November 1932 for the Trowbridge service.

Preparing for Further Growth

Lavington & Devizes Motor Services Ltd was registered on 17 November 1922 and was formed to acquire and carry on the business of motor omnibuses, coaches, hackney carriages and garage proprietors. In addition to Frederick Sayer of Market Lavington, the directors were Harry, Alfred and Fred Chivers, all of Devizes. They were part of a nationally known dynasty of haulage contractors, builders and craftsmen.

William Edward Chivers was born at Avebury in 1855. At the age of fifteen he walked to Devizes to be apprenticed as a carpenter to his cousin Jabez Chivers. He eventually set up his own carpentry business in 1884, gaining a good local reputation. In 1906 his activities were diversified more strongly into general building work and also ground works. In due course, all nine of his sons were apprenticed to their father as carpenters. Chivers bought the former Brown & May engineering premises in Estcourt Street, Devizes, in November 1913, while further diversification included monumental and stonework, a sawmill, sanitary engineering and a builders' merchants. A large workforce was developed. Major construction projects were undertaken as a preferred contractor to the War Department and a fleet of 200 steam wagons and traction engines was built up, as well as motor lorries and several hundred horses, used for own-account activities as well as for general haulage.

William Chivers died in February 1916, aged sixty-one; the family firm was then controlled by oldest son Frederick (Fred). W. E. Chivers & Sons Ltd was formed in March 1919, with six of the sons as directors, including Fred, Henry (Harry) and Alfred. Quarrying, coal extraction and furniture removal were yet more of their commercial interests. By the 1920s the company was a prosperous and respected concern, with work and branches in various parts of the UK. In September 1922, the old Devizes prison was acquired; the curious public were admitted on payment of 1s, with the proceeds donated to the local hospital. The building was then dismantled and the stone used in new houses being built by Chivers in Avon View. Around the same time, the firm's directors invested in other local property as well as in Lavington & Devizes Motor Services Ltd. Hence this small detour into the history of probably the best-known business based in Devizes in the twentieth century, apart perhaps from Wadworth's Brewery.

Established 1884.

ON ADMIRALTY & WAR OFFICE LISTS.

W. E. CHIVERS & SONS,

BUILDERS, CONTRACTORS,

TIMBER & BUILDERS' MERCHANTS.

JOINERY MANUFACTURERS.

Traction Motor & Horse Transport Contractors

North Wilts Building & Electric Joinery Works,

DEVIZES.

Works cover 2½ Acres.

Sand and Gravel Pits, Romsey,

Branches:

BULFORD CAMP	Salisbury Plain	Bulford Telephone...	..	47
TIDWORTH and		Cholderton ..	...	10
NETHERAVON		Tidworth .,	...	67
ROMSEY and WINCHESTER.		Romsey ..	...	52

Head Office, Devizes. Telephone 121 & 122.

(Private Branch Exchange)

Left: Directory listing for W. E. Chivers & Sons, 1916.

Below: HR 4065 was a Commer WP1, first registered in April 1921. It had left the fleet by mid-1924, so may not have been converted to run on air-filled rubber tyres. (MLM)

Fred Chivers was the eldest son, called a spade a spade and loved gadgets. Seeking the latest thing on offer, he insisted that W. E. Chivers & Sons should have one of the first tower cranes in the UK. After King Edward VIII abdicated, Fred purchased his Buick car, complete with tinted windows. He served for twenty-five years on Devizes Town Council, was an alderman for ten years and was mayor in 1925/6. He worked hard to raise funds for the local hospital and to support the Devizes Carnival. In 1932 he became president of the Chamber of Commerce and died in 1942, a true pillar of municipal and community life. Harry Chivers was described as being a strict disciplinarian, but generous. Interested in sport, he was chairman of Devizes Town Football Club and the Wiltshire Football Association. Alfred Chivers had little time for outside interests – he devoted all his energy to the business and was its driving force, like his father before him.

The first board meeting of L&DMS Ltd was held on 18 December 1922 at 20 Estcourt Street, Devizes – the premises of W. E. Chivers & Sons. Sayer was elected chairman and Edmund Bull was appointed secretary. The latter was released as trustee of a provisional agreement of 20 October 1922. The registered office was 9 Bank Chambers, Devizes – Bull's office address. London Joint City & Midland Bank Ltd was selected as the firm's banker; as William Chivers's firm had built the Devizes branch and was its first customer, this was not surprising! Sayer was to subscribe to 1,500 £1 7 5 per cent cumulative preference shares and 1,500 ordinary shares. Each of the Chivers was to subscribe to 500 preference and ordinary shares. Sayer's freehold property at Market Lavington was to be vested in the company and £6,000 was to be borrowed as additional capital, secured by a debenture trust deed dated 14 February 1923, charged on the company's land, premises and other assets. By the end of December it was resolved that authorised capital be increased to £10,000, of which £9,000 was issued.

By November 1922, further bus service changes had taken place. The Market Lavington–Devizes–Bath service of L&DMS was running on Thursdays, making it a daily operation, while Bath Tramways Motor Co. was also running Bath–Devizes on Mondays, Tuesdays, Wednesdays and Fridays, departing at 2.30 p.m. and returning at 4.15 p.m., in addition to Thursdays and Sundays. A Sunday service of two afternoon/evening round trips had been introduced on Market Lavington–Trowbridge, which diverted via Great Cheverell. The Pewsey service had been withdrawn on Wednesdays except for one journey into Devizes, which ran through to Bath via Melksham, leaving at 9 a.m. and returning at 5 p.m.

Once again the commercial photographer captured the whole charabanc during the morning stop in Salisbury. HR 6676 was one of six Crossley X-type fourteen-seat charabancs put on the road by L&DMS in 1921/2, with reconditioned older chassis. (R. Grimley Collection)

Yet another of the Crossleys was HR 7538, dating from November 1922. Of the two drivers, the one on the right is thought to be 'Tubby' Cooper. (MLM)

Although this invoice was printed in the time when Fred Sayer was sole proprietor, the transaction took place in 1923 after formation of the limited company. To supplement the bus and charabanc activities, L&DMS also undertook general motor repairs and the supply of parts. The Market Lavington Estate had bought two brass bushes for a piece of machinery for 7s 6d. (MLM)

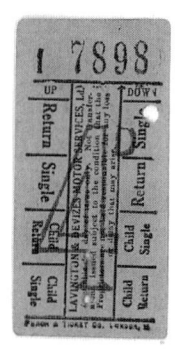

A selection of tickets issued over the years by L&DMS.

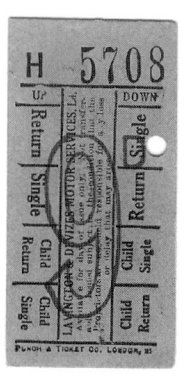

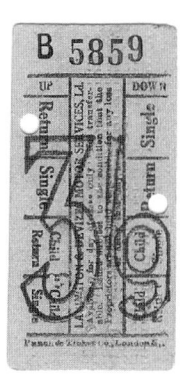

Moving South – Halls of Orcheston

In January 1923 the newly raised capital allowed the acquisition of the business of another bus operator, C. E. & C. H. Hall, trading as Hall & Son of Orcheston. This village is south of Devizes across Salisbury Plain, so once again L&DMS territory was enlarged. It was reported at the 26 January L&DMS board meeting that an agreement had been concluded for the transfer of operations, goodwill, the tenancy of a garage at Orcheston, a freehold house in Salisbury, vehicles and other assets.

John Hall, born in 1858, was a farm bailiff who became the landlord of the Crown Inn at Orcheston St George. By 1895 he was the village carrier, carrying on an essential function that had, since at least the 1860s, been performed by Messrs Smith, Axford, Dewey and Smith, in that order. From the Orcheston, Maddington and Shrewton area he ran to Salisbury on Tuesdays and Saturdays, using the yard of the Shoulder of Mutton in St Thomas's Square in Salisbury as stabling and as a parcel collection point. On Thursdays he headed north over Salisbury Plain to Devizes for the market, which no doubt was challenging for man and beast in bad weather.

In October 1912, Hall took delivery of what was claimed to be the first motor vehicle for the conveyance of passengers and goods in the Salisbury area – a twenty-seat 3-ton bus registered AM 2708. This was built by Scout Motors, a company based in Salisbury and run by Albert Burden. The vehicle had ball-bearing transmission and was driven by a chain enclosed in a large aluminium guard. There were windows at the side and rear and a luggage grid on the roof for carrying all the produce and goods to and from the markets. Several of the other carriers running into Salisbury purchased Scout vehicles around this time and the local press described this as 'the revolution in rural road travel'. In 1915 the workshop machinery at the Scout factory was requisitioned for use in France, to be replaced by the enforced production of munitions. Vehicle manufacture could not be recommenced until 1920, but by then the firm faced severe foreign competition; the company was wound up in June 1921.

Trading as Shrewton Motor Service, Hall ran his Scout vehicle on Tuesdays and Saturdays into Salisbury from Orcheston via Shrewton, Winterbourne Stoke, Berwick St James, Stapleford, Stoford, South Newton and Wilton. On Thursdays the route was from Salisbury back the same way to Shrewton and then across the Plain to Tilshead, Gore

This is thought to be the first charabanc bought by the Hall family, in 1913. AM 3059 had seating for twenty-seven, and the chassis was built locally, by the Scout company in Salisbury. The location is the Plume of Feathers public house at Shrewton on 10 January 1914. Scout products encouraged several carriers in the area to start conversion from horse to motor traction. It is about to set off with football enthusiasts who were going to watch Swindon Town play Manchester United – no women allowed, and hats or caps obligatory! Swindon beat Manchester United 1-0. Perhaps the dog is upset at not being allowed to go as well. How many of these men never returned from the impending worldwide conflict? (D. J. N. Pennels Collection)

Halls' Shrewton Motor Service took delivery in November 1915 of this Scout, registered AM 5363, with bodywork appropriate for their bus/carrier services from Devizes and Orcheston into Salisbury. The two men may be Clifford and Charles Hall. (D. J. N. Pennels Collection)

Cross, West Lavington, Littleton Panell and Potterne into Devizes. In 1913 a twenty-seven-seat Scout charabanc (AM 3054) arrived, but John Hall died in June of that year. The business passed to his widow Martha Hall, née Smith, who was born at Orcheston St Mary in 1862. She was assisted by her sons Clifford Edmond and Charles Henry, although there were eleven other offspring! On 15 April 1914, the family celebrated a double wedding at Orcheston St George. Agnes Hall married Louis Chant and Clifford Hall married Eva Grist. These were the first weddings in the village for which a motor car was used to transport the brides. In early 1917, Margaret Hall married Charlie Sparrow, who was to become a partner in Victory Motor Services, a substantial Salisbury-based competitor for Wilts & Dorset Motor Services. The Sparrows lived at 2 Nelson Road, Salisbury, this being the property acquired by L&DMS with the Hall business.

In November 1915 the Hall brothers purchased another Scout – a twenty-six-seat bus registered AM 5363 – and in the following October a five-seat Scout 'torpedo' car (MR 4250). Not long after the end of the war, in 1919, the Halls started a Tuesday and Saturday service into Salisbury from Hindon via Berwick St Leonard, Fonthill Bishop, Chilmark, Teffont Magna, Dinton, Barford St Martin, Burcombe, Ugford and Wilton. This route was to be contested during the 1920s and early 1930s by a number of small operators. The pioneer was Frederick Rawlings in 1913, with a service from East Knoyle and Hindon into Salisbury on Tuesdays and Saturdays using a Scout motor

The Charabanc at the rear was HR 170, an AEC YC type with thirty-two seats, delivered in July 1919 and used also on Halls' Hindon–Salisbury bus service. At the front is HR 1004, a Daimler CK with twenty-six seats, introduced in January 1920 on a 1918 chassis acquired from the War Department. The location is outside Parson's shop at 37 Devizes Road, Salisbury. (Peter Daniels Photo Archive)

vehicle. From January 1922, Rawlings and the Halls had competition from Fred and Reg Viney, who ran a former War Department Ford Model T lorry fitted with seats from Chilmark to Salisbury on Tuesdays, Thursdays and Saturdays.

During 1919, Halls initiated replacement of their Scout vehicles with two AEC YC-type charabancs (AM 9371 and 9574) and an AEC YC with thirty-two seats and described as a 'Pullman bus' (HR 89). Another AEC YC charabanc (HR 170) was at one time out-stationed in a garage at Hindon, to operate the service thence to Salisbury. These were followed by two vehicles (or at least their chassis) acquired from the War Department and then registered in Wiltshire – HR 1004, a twenty-six-seat Daimler CK charabanc, in January 1920 and HR 4010, a fourteen-seat Crossley X-type charabanc, in May 1921. By 1920, Halls were also running into Devizes on Saturdays. In that year, Martha Hall passed away, leaving Clifford and Charles in charge. From 26 September 1921, now trading as Salisbury, Shrewton & Devizes Motor Services, they commenced running a through service from Salisbury to Devizes every day of the week. The journey took about two hours, with departures from Salisbury at 9.15 a.m. and 3.15 p.m. and from Devizes at 9.00 a.m. and 3.15 p.m. On Fridays and Saturdays there was an extra journey at 5.50 p.m. from each end of the route, although adjustments to evening journeys took place as soon as 18 November 1921, when the Sunday service ceased too. In addition there was still one round trip on Tuesdays from Orcheston via Shrewton into Salisbury and two on Saturdays, including an evening facility returning at 10.30 p.m.

The final new vehicle delivered was a 40 hp Dennis bus, believed to have carried a thirty-two-seat body by Dodson and registered HR 5593 in November 1921. This vehicle, together with the four AECs, the Daimler and the bus services, passed to L&DMS on 8 January 1923. L&D also acquired the use of the garage next to the Crown Inn at Orcheston, which was leased from the brewery.

Another view of the Daimler HR 1004, this time with AM 9371, another AEC YC type charabanc once owned by the Halls. The occasion is an outing for staff at Wadworth's Brewery in Devizes, and may have been subsequent to the takeover of these two vehicles, along with the Hall business, by L&DMS. (L. Tancock Collection)

The Heyday of the Company

Apart from the former Hall vehicles, several others were introduced by L&DMS during 1923. There was AM 8761, a thirty-two-seat Commer RC bus on a 1917 former War Department chassis, and HR 8651, another fourteen-seat Crossley X-type charabanc, possibly from the same source. In March, the BTMC board minutes suggest that there was an agreement for them to supply L&DMS with two Commer vehicles in exchange for two AEC chassis that Fred Sayer had acquired. These Commer WP1s appear to have been FB 045, a twenty-seven-seat charabanc that L&DMS later converted into a lorry, and FB 051, with a Dodson/BET body that was apparently replaced by Sayer with one purchased from Wilts & Dorset. Demonstrating further his resourcefulness, Sayer constructed another charabanc (LX 8276) utilising the AEC YC-type chassis of a former London & South Western Railway lorry.

By September 1923, possibly from 1 June, the Market Lavington–Bath via Erlestoke service had gained a round trip on Saturday afternoons, departing at 1.45 p.m. and returning at 8 p.m., while the Chippenham service was also running on Tuesdays and Saturdays. With operations increasing and the need for a booking office facility for coach excursions and private hire in Devizes, agreement was reached in early 1923 for the lease of 59–61 Northgate Street, near the Market Place, from Messrs Anstie & Leaf. It was reported in November that year that W. Hayward, who occupied part of the premises privately, had let some rooms to act as an office for the Liberal Party candidate at the December election. He had allowed election posters to be displayed. The board resolved that these should be removed and that company vehicles and premises should not be used in future for any political purposes. 59 Northgate Street was listed as the office of East Wilts Liberal Association, with Hayward's name, as early as 1916.

Although L&DMS got much of the local private hire business, there was competition in Potterne. By spring 1923, H. S. Wells, who had a general motor garage in the High Street, was advertising a fourteen-seat charabanc for hire, as well as cars. He provided a carrier service on Tuesdays, Thursdays and Saturdays to and from Devizes.

There do not seem to have been any significant L&DMS service changes in 1924, although by February that year a Sunday service had been reinstated on the Devizes–

This is the garage behind Ivydene in Market Lavington. The vehicle is FB045, a Commer WP1 noted as acquired from Bath Tramways Motor Co. in July 1923 and recorded as a charabanc. Here, it appears with a lorry body – it is known that such body changes occurred on some vehicles as needs required. Left to right are seen Fred Sayer junior, Mabel Sayer looking cross, the substantial Fred Sayer senior, John Cooper (village blacksmith), Harry Hobbs, George Hobbs and Charlie Sheppard, as well as Jaky the dog. (MLM)

Outside The Roebuck Inn (licensee A. Runyeard), believed to be in Weymouth, is Crossley HR 5028, dating from July 1921. (MLM)

Salisbury route, with two journeys each way, and the journeys operated by BTMC on Mondays, Tuesdays, Wednesdays and Fridays between Bath, Melksham and Devizes had disappeared from the timetable. On the vehicle front, Sayer introduced the first of several AEC 502-type vehicles which were rebuilt over a three-year period. These vehicles have been described as being built from components or 'spare parts'. Another theory is that they may have been old AEC Y-type chassis acquired from various sources and then upgraded to the equivalent of the 502-type with a conversion kit supplied by AEC. Whatever, they were probably another advantageous solution for expanding the fleet very economically. The first three (MR 862/3/5) were ready by May 1924 and were twenty-eight or thirty-two-seat 'all-weather' vehicles with folding canvas roofs – a cross between what is generally described as a charabanc and a coach. They were certainly welcome for handling the burgeoning pleasure trip traffic. Also put on the road in 1924 were MR 58, an all-weather coach with a 1917 vintage former AEC YC lorry chassis acquired from the W. E. Chivers haulage fleet, and XM 867, a similar vehicle with a 1918 lorry chassis.

Before the advent of the National Health Service after the Second World War, communities put much effort into raising money for local hospitals and other care facilities so that those without their own means could still receive medical treatment. There was a Lavington and Easterton Hospital Week, with a carnival-style day and several other fund-raising competitions with an entry fee. In 1923, Fred Sayer contributed a prize for the Tombola Draw – some free seats on a charabanc excursion to Bournemouth, which were won by Emily Shepherd of White Street in Market Lavington. In 1924 there was a competition to guess the combined weight of six men from the village, with 'handsome prizes' offered for the nearest correct guess. Fred Sayer was a somewhat large man, so he duly appeared as one of the six. Mabel Sayer also entered into the spirit of the occasion by dressing up in a fancy costume at fundraising carnival events. Another Crossley car was registered to her in January 1924; its number plate, MR 1, would be very valuable today.

By 1924 the supposed combined capacity of the L&DMS fleet allowed the company to advertise open and closed vehicles for hire, seating parties of fourteen to 600, under the title of Green Motor Coaches. As well as the usual coastal trips and Tidworth Military Tattoo, there were excursions to places such as Southampton on 24 June, to see the Prince of Wales opening the new floating dock, the extremely popular British Empire Exhibition at Wembley and the somewhat static delights of the Frome Cheese Show in September. A typical weekly excursion programme, such as for early September 1924, consisted of Bournemouth on Tuesday and Friday (which became almost a regular once or twice weekly seasonal 'service' featuring period return fares valid up to fourteen days), Oxford (for St Giles' Fair), Wembley, Cheddar and Weston-super-Mare and Longleat House, the latter in the days long before lions and other animals were featured, unlike the 1970s when many coaches in southern and western England had a sticker displayed inside stating 'We have seen the Lions of Longleat'! The principal picking up points were Market Lavington and Devizes and seats could be booked at the company's offices in those two places, the Shrewton office (i.e. at Orcheston) and at Mrs Oliver's newsagent's shop at 19 The Brittox, Devizes. In addition, to cater for

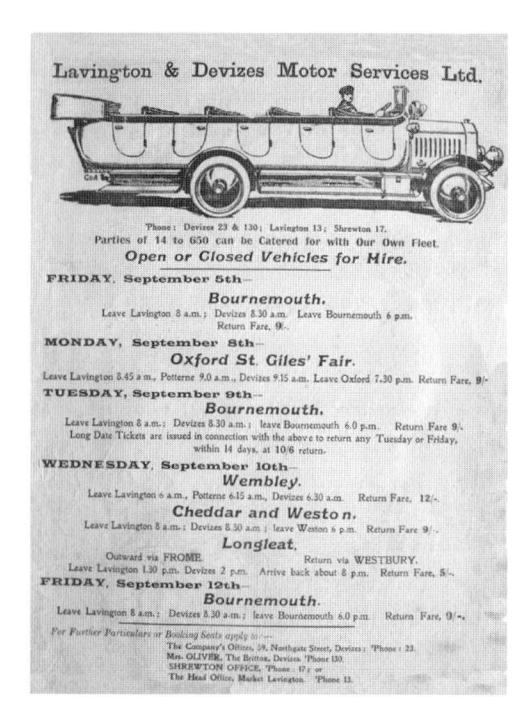

The L&DMS excursion programme for early September 1924, as printed in the local newspaper, has a drawing of a charabanc, but by then several improved 'all-weather' coaches were in the fleet. The Bournemouth trip ran twice a week during each summer season, while the Wembley trip was probably for the British Empire Exhibition. (MLM)

pleasure trips on a rare day of rest for the working man, there was a full service on the bus routes on Bank Holiday Mondays, including four trips from Market Lavington and five from Devizes to Bath and back again.

Most trips to the southern coastal resorts, such as Bournemouth or Weymouth, featured a refreshment and comfort stop at Salisbury in each direction. In New Canal, an enterprising photographer would take a group photo of the many charabanc parties in the morning and then spend the day developing prints so he could sell them to the passengers in postcard form for around 3*d* each during the evening stop. The main purpose was to encourage those in the picture to buy one; therefore, sadly, he rarely captured the front of the vehicle and its registration number, to aid identification. However, that is largely why we are able to include images of various L&DMS charabanc parties in this book. In the 1920s and 1930s summer seasons, photographer Harold Whitworth would be there with his bicycle and a parrot or similar on his shoulder. One of his birds is remembered as squawking rude but amusing utterances about Adolf Hitler.

L&DMS was appointed as the road transport agent for the Great Western Railway's rail/road inclusive day excursions to Stonehenge, Old Sarum and surrounding district. A large number of passengers (perhaps as many as 230–270) would disembark at Lavington station from special trains at weekends and then be transported onwards over the Plain by a significant proportion of the L&DMS charabanc and all-weather coach fleet; such activity looked very impressive, with the yard of the station full of vehicles, which then set off in convoy.

However, as early as January 1925, the Chivers family directors had concerns about some of the company's expenditure. Sayer was instructed to approach Mrs Hayward, who ran the Devizes office on an agency basis, to see if she would accept reduced payment of £1 per week and rent-free occupation of the remainder of 59 Northgate Street. However, it was important to have an office in the town as other firms were competing for excursion business. One example was H. Burry's Wilsford Motor Service, who used T. Nash of 1 Wharf Street as his agent. From 23 June 1925 he was offering an excursion to Bournemouth every Tuesday from Devizes via Wilsford, Rushall, Enford, Netheravon and Amesbury. The L&D directors required that savings were also sought in wages paid; for some time the rate was 7s 6d a week for conductors and £2 for drivers. It was noted that the inspector was to become a driver/mechanic, with a reduction in remuneration. Some of his duties were to be performed periodically instead by George Watson O'Reilly. George was living in Canada at the outbreak of war but immediately returned to England to enlist in the army. After being demobilised, he came to work for Fred Sayer in 1920 and was a valued member of staff as a driver and in a supervisory capacity.

Entering the fleet in 1925 were four more re-constructed 'AEC 502s' – two with thirty-two-seat saloon bus bodies (MR 2468/9) and two more all-weather coaches (MR3575/6). To raise revenue, a contract was entered into with Messrs Abrahams for the latter to buy to let advertising space inside fifteen buses for three years and this was followed in early 1926 by a further deal whereby Abrahams would take twenty-four advert spaces on four fourteen-seat charabancs for £8 for an eight-month period.

In 1924–5, L&DMS constructed ten all-weather coaches or saloon buses, using bought-in AEC components and/or reconditioned chassis, economical home-made versions described as being either of the AEC YC type or the 502 type. They replaced some of the early Commers. MR 2468 was one of a pair with bus bodies registered in January 1925, out in the countryside on the Devizes–Pewsey service. The driver is Charlie Sheppard (seen earlier with Commers HR 655 and FB 045) and the conductor is Jack Boulton. It was a shame that the photographer did not frame the shot better, but it's all we have! (L. Tancock Collection)

The increasing size of the fleet outstripped the capacity of the garage next to Ivydene. During the 1920s, the attractive and substantial 'Doctor's House' (originally the home of a maltster), on the north side of the marketplace, was partially demolished; this had been an elegant Georgian structure. Being in close proximity to Ivydene, L&DMS had secured the site as an additional bus parking area, along with the adjacent premises previously used by builder Arthur Oatley, who had a car for hire as early as 1915. A section of the original front wall of the house was incorporated into new brickwork at the front of the premises and a pair of high wooden gates was installed. In later years, the surviving windows of the old house were boarded over and painted lettering appeared exhorting one to 'Travel by Bus' and 'Travel by Coach'. In January 1924, the Parish Council noted that L&DMS had made some repairs to the road surface in the marketplace – where it had deteriorated in places, it was described as 'almost like a ploughed field'. As the L&DMS fleet became larger, even more parking space than that available in the marketplace was required, so some vehicles were also kept at Holloway Bros. brickworks on Broadway, north of the village, according to one source.

On 2 September 1924 at 6.30 p.m., William Jolliffe of New Park Street, Devizes, was attempting to board an L&DMS bus on the Bath service that was already moving away from the stop in Devizes Market Place. The vehicle struck him and he fell to the ground. He was taken to hospital and although no bones were apparently broken, it was reported in the press that serious internal injuries were feared.

In a somewhat vain attempt to search for some new custom, perhaps seeking trade from military establishments on the Plain, Wilts & Dorset Motor Services experimented with various rural services including some that originated in the Wylye Valley at Codford, north-west of Salisbury on the Warminster road. In December 1921 they had started a Wednesday service to Frome via Warminster. This was followed by a route to Devizes on Thursdays from April 1922, and one on Tuesdays into Salisbury. These were eventually numbered 5B, 5C and 5 respectively but they did not prove particularly successful. They had passed by June 1925 (quite possibly the previous year) to L&DMS, although to complicate matters, they were not listed among Wilts & Dorset services in the Travel By Road (TBR) timetable booklet after May 1923, but for that matter, they were not included in the L&DMS entries either, up to the last edition of TBR in 1924! These services were somewhat divorced from L&DMS primary territory, so the vehicle was out-stationed at Codford, as Wilts & Dorset had been. The W&D vehicle previously allocated was transferred to more remunerative activities elsewhere. The services were: Codford–Wylye–Steeple Langford–Stapleford–Stoford–South Newton–Wilton–Salisbury (Tuesdays and Saturdays); Codford–Heytesbury–Warminster–Crockerton–Horningsham–Woodlands-Frome (Wednesdays); Codford–Heytesbury–Warminster–Imber–Gore Cross–West Lavington–Littleton Panell–Potterne–Devizes (Thursdays). L&D then had three services into Salisbury – those from Devizes/Orcheston and from Hindon, acquired from Halls and the one from Codford.

A new excursion was advertised in 1925 and in subsequent years, featuring frequently in the seasonal programme. The half-day circular tour from Market Lavington and Devizes took in Farleigh Castle and allowed a stay in Bath of one and a half hours. A

Tuesdays, Wednesdays, Fridays and Saturdays.

	A.M.		P.M	P.M				A.M.		P.M.	P.M	
Bath Guildhall d	11 0	....	310	7 0	....	Calne............... d	9 10	....	1 20	510	....
Bathford	1114	....	324	714	....	Sandy Lane	9 22	....	1 32	522	....
Farleigh Wick	1125	....	335	725	....	Westbrook N.Inn	9 28	....	1 38	528	....
Bradford (C. Inn)	1135	....	345	735	....	Melksham	9 45	....	1 55	545	....
Holt	1147	....	357	747	....	Br'ghton G F.R	9 55	....	2 5	555	....
Br'ghton G. F. R.	1155	....	4 5	755	....	Holt	10 3	....	2 13	6 3	....
Melksham	12 5	....	415	8 5	....	Bradford (C. Inn)	1015	....	2 25	615	....
Westbrook N.Inn	1222	....	432	822	....	Farleigh Wick	1025	....	2 35	625	....
Sandy Lane	1228	......	438	828	......	Bathford	1036	......	2 46	636	......
Calne .... a	1240	......	450	840	......	**Bath Guildhall** a	1050	......	3 0	650	......

Sundays.

	P.M			P.M				P.M			P.M	
Bath Guildhall d	2 0	420	......	6 0	815	.....	Calne................d	130	340	.....	615	815	.....
Bathford	214	434	......	614	829	.....	Studley	143	353	.....	628	828	.....
Box Station	222	442	......	622	837	.....	Chippenham	2 0	410	.....	645	845	.....
Box Post Office	225	445	......	625	840	.....	Corsham Town H	220	430	.....	7 5	9 5	.....
Pickwick	237	457	......	637	852	.....	Pickwick	223	433	.....	7 8	9 8	.....
Corsham Town H	240	5 0	......	640	855	.....	Box Post Office	235	445	.....	720	920	.....
Chippenham	3 0	520	......	7 0	915	.....	Box Station	238	448	.....	723	923	.....
Studley	317	537	......	717	932	.....	Bathford	246	456	.....	731	931	.....
Calne................a	330	550	......	730	945	.....	**Bath Guildhall**...a	3 0	510	.....	745	945	.....

The Bath–Calne services, as shown in L&DMS's own timetable booklet.

Early in 1926 it seems that L&DMS were approached by Edwin Cave of Upavon Motor Services regarding buying his business. In 1913 Cave used this Scout vehicle, registered AM 2882, to motorise his carrier runs to Salisbury, Pewsey and Devizes, but it is pictured here on a weekend outing to Bournemouth. (D. J. N. Pennels Collection)

Cave's somewhat austere Dennis, registered HR 760, new in November 1919, with solid tyres and open sides may have come into the L&DMS fleet if the takeover had gone ahead, but the directors of that company declined the opportunity. (D. J. N. Pennels Collection)

Opposite: Crossley X-type fourteen-seat charabanc HR 5028 again, photographed in around 1926 in Salisbury, during a short break on the way to Weymouth. Harry Hobbs was the driver, and his future wife Betty Pike was among the party. (MLM)

stop was made at the Glasshouse Café at Combe Down, owned by BET, where tea was provided, being included in the 5s fare.

The Chivers brothers and Fred Sayer met for a board meeting on 25 February 1926. It was noted that purchase of E. G. Cave's business would not be entertained, although had the services been acquired, it would have consolidated the eastern side of L&D's territory. In the early 1900s, Edwin Cave of Upavon, east of Devizes, took over a carrier business from his father, George Cave. With a horse and van, he went to Salisbury, Marlborough and Devizes. Motorisation came in 1913 with purchase of a Scout saloon bus registered AM 2882. By the early 1920s, Cave was trading as Upavon Motor Services and by May 1922 he had bus routes from Pewsey to Salisbury via Upavon on Tuesdays and Saturdays (with a feeder service on Tuesdays from Woodborough), and from Netheravon to Devizes on Thursdays via Upavon and Charlton. There was also an evening round trip from Upavon to Devizes on Saturdays, useful for cinema patrons. A reinstatement of a pre-war service from Upavon to Marlborough via Woodborough on Mondays, but extended to Swindon, had only lasted from 21 August 1922 until 29 January 1923. Charabancs were used for excursions and private hire and cars were available for hire as well. Following L&DMS's refusal to purchase in 1926, operations passed subsequently to William Charles Mortimer of Upavon, trading as Upavon & District. However, the Devizes and Salisbury routes were sold by Mortimer on 28 November 1932 to Wilts & Dorset, who integrated them into their own existing services.

Other matters discussed revealed that tickets were not issued by L&DMS to passengers as they boarded the bus – fare collection and ticket issue may well have been on alighting. The directors decided this should be reversed forthwith. The net profit of £173 5s 11d for the year ending September 1925 was seen as disappointing.

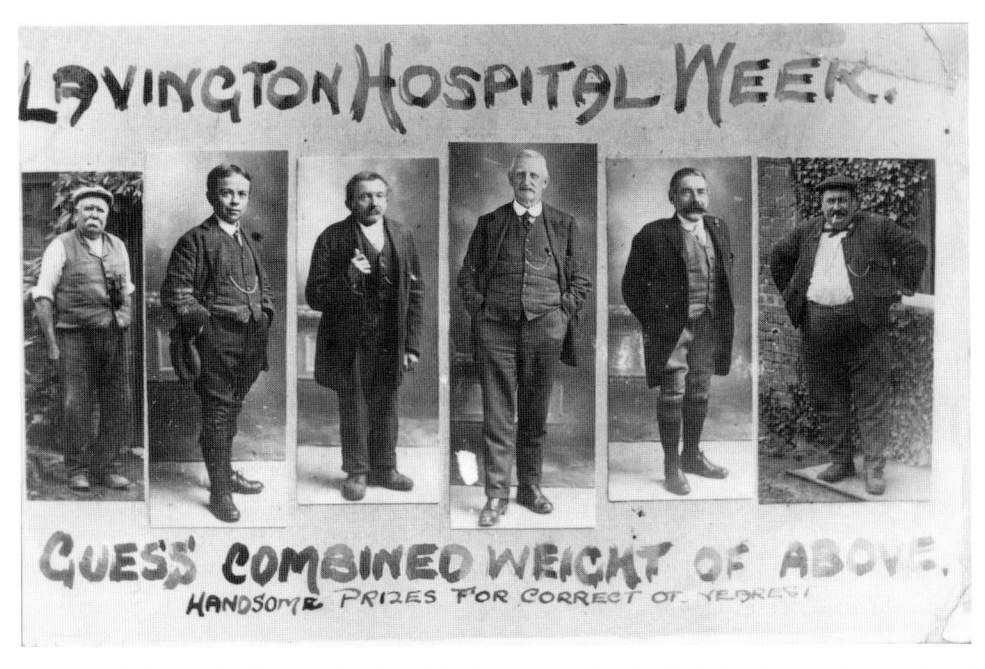

As part of charity fundraising for the 1926 Lavington Hospital Week, a 'guess the combined weight of these six men' competition was organised. Left to right were Dan Perrett, Freddy Chapman, Billy Topp, James Welch, William Elisha and, of course, Fred Sayer. (MLM)

For several years, Mabel Sayer joined in with the carnival spirit by collecting money for the local hospital while in fancy dress. This is most likely her Florence Nightingale impression. (MLM)

Fred Sayer was required to supply each vehicle's earnings and thought was to be given to reducing journeys on the Pewsey, Chippenham and 'Shrewton' services. In due course the Pewsey–Devizes service was reduced to run only on Thursdays, Saturdays and Sundays. This and other adjustments resulted in a weekly mileage saving of 324 (Pewsey), 60 for Salisbury, 145 for Shrewton and 48 on Trowbridge. The Chippenham service was to be worked with a Fiat twenty-seat bus which also covered a service that only operated on days that Devizes Secondary School was in session. This started at Market Lavington and served Easterton, Urchfont, Chirton, Patney, All Cannings, Allington and Horton. The Fiat may have been MO 2406, which was acquired from Denham Bros. of Newbury. Wiltshire County Council made payments to L&DMS for the conveyance of 'free place' pupils to Devizes Secondary School at a rate of 6*d* per child per day; this was increased to 8*d* in November 1928.

Other changes saw the Hindon to Salisbury service increased, with a Monday–Saturday round trip for shopping and an additional evening facility at weekends. The vehicle for this service was garaged at Hindon by L&DMS, as it had been by Halls. The resident driver was Frank Grist, who was probably related to Eva Grist, who had married Clifford Hall. Some private hire work was obtained from the Hindon area,

Conductor Stan Weston and driver Jack Boulton stand in front of AEC Y-type saloon bus NR 3128, the chassis at least of which was registered in Leicestershire in 1923 and acquired from a dealer called Aldridge around the mid-1920s. (L. Tancock Collection)

A group of L&DMS staff with an unidentified saloon bus, possibly in Devizes marketplace. (L. Tancock Collection)

for which a vehicle had to be sent from Orcheston or Market Lavington. By May 1926 journeys on the Market Lavington–Devizes service were advertised in the BTMC timetable booklet as running via Easterton and Urchfont on Sundays, a day when Laurence Tom Alexander of Lydeway (trading as Queen of the Road) did not operate. From the same year, or possibly from their introduction on 11 July 1925, it seems that some sort of arrangement had been agreed whereby L&DMS operated the BTMC services between Bath and Calne, although some mystery surrounds the circumstances. Contemporary local timetables do not refer to the operator and BTMC's own make no reference to L&DMS. The services may have been worked on behalf of BTMC or they may have been jointly operated, but they would have required significant dead-running from/to the depot at Market Lavington, or maybe vehicles were out-stationed at Bath and Calne. There may be a clue in references in Bath Watch Committee records: later, in June 1930, it was noted that a vehicle licence was transferred from Bath Tramways Motor IJ 5353 (AEC 503) to HR 89, an ex-Halls AEC YC. Similarly, noted in February 1931 was the transfer of a BTMC licence from HR 6676 (Crossley) to MW 8248 (Lancia). As the latter three, at least, were actually L&DMS vehicles, it may have been expedient for some reason for them to be licensed by BTMC if they were based in Bath, perhaps for the Calne services. In any case, L&D's own timetables show three journeys each way from Calne to Bath on Tuesdays, Wednesdays, Fridays and Saturdays via

This twenty-seat Fiat bus (MO 2406) is thought to have been acquired by L&DMS from Denham Bros of Newbury by 1926, and was apparently used on the Devizes school service from Market Lavington and various villages to the east of Devizes, as well as on the service to Chippenham. It was first registered in December 1923, and was converted to a lorry by July 1931, after which it survived with L&DMS and BTMC until 1933. (P. Lacey Collection)

Sandy Lane, Westbrook, Melksham, Holt, Woolley Green, Bradford on Avon, Farleigh Wick and Bathford. On Sundays, the route was via Studley, Swan Inn, Chippenham, Corsham, Pickwick, Rudloe, Box and Bathford, with four journeys each way. All this may point to further cooperation between L&D and BTMC.

As well as the Fiat mentioned earlier, 1926 saw the introduction of some more buses – two more rebuilt AEC 502s (MR 5600/1), a Crossley (MR 5675) and a 1920 AEC YA registered L 6476, acquired from South Wales Commercial Motors. No doubt the extensive fleet was fully deployed on occasions such as Wednesday 1 September 1926, when many extra bus service journeys and pre-bookable trips were run from the L&DMS area into Devizes for the carnival, military tattoo, fireworks display and dance. There was even a late journey back to Market Lavington at the conclusion of the dance at 2 a.m.

The accounts for the year ending September 1926 showed a loss of £51 3*s* 3*d* after debenture interest and depreciation. Thereafter the company never showed a profit; despite their prosperity, the Chivers brothers were probably increasingly worried.

In the mid-1920s, probably in Salisbury, we see former Halls AEC YC-type HR 170, which by then had acquired pneumatic tyres and saloon bus bodywork to replace the former charabanc body. The driver was Albert Froud, who worked for L&DMS from 1925 to 1928, and the conductor was George Fox. It often took both of them to turn the large starting handle at the front. (R. Grimley Collection)

A Downward Slide

With a pressing need for financial prudence, there was little ability for L&DMS to expand. The acquisition of only two vehicles has been dated to 1927. These were HF 1743, an AEC YC with thirty-two-seat bus bodywork by Hora, in February and MR 9504, a new ADC 416A bus with bodywork by Brush, in June. The AEC had been previously operated by Wallasey Corporation Transport, but was new to the Liverpool municipal fleet in October 1919, when it was registered KB 1967. The ADC, however, was contemporary and probably lifted the morale of those involved with L&DMS. In the following year, 1928, it was back to frugality with the introduction of MW 1577, which was an old AEC Y-type chassis acquired from a dealer, rebuilt and given a bus body, possibly by Dodson, which had been purchased from Wilts & Dorset.

In spring 1927, the death of BET's and BTMC's respected general manager and a director, William Hardy, was recorded. His place on the boards was filled by John Roney, who became a principal director of the companies. Interestingly, Roney was also a director and the secretary of the Ceara Tramway Light & Power Co. Ltd in Brazil, while fellow long-serving Bath director and chairman Evelyn Trenow was chairman of the South American concern. Also in October 1927, BTMC decided to give numbers to their bus services; relevant to the L&D story, Bath–Melksham–Calne was numbered 8, Bath–Chippenham–Calne 9 and Bath–Melksham–Devizes 13.

Sometime between 1927 and April 1929, the Devizes–Chippenham service became a daily operation, although certain buses ran through from/to Market Lavington on Saturdays and Sundays. Those journeys to Salisbury that started from Orcheston were running Mondays to Saturdays by July 1928, while by July 1929 the Codford–Salisbury service had gained a Sunday afternoon journey into the city, returning at 9.30 p.m. and the weekday journeys from Market Lavington to Trowbridge ran via Great Cheverell in line with those on Sundays.

One of the L&DMS drivers was Henry Charles Hobbs, born in February 1902 at Shoreditch in London. His parents lived at the Workmens' Hall in Market Lavington, where his mother was the caretaker. Harry also had additional duties for L&DMS. Apparently, Fred Sayer found it very hard to get to sleep on occasion; the only remedy was for him to be driven around the area in a car, in which he would soon be snoring.

By now on proper pneumatic tyres, this unidentified charabanc was probably seen in the latter half of the 1920s. It may have been one of several AEC Y-series models in the fleet. (MLM)

This was Harry's late night task and once back at Ivydene, he would switch off the engine and get out quietly, leaving Fred to sleep. Harry's bus driving career eventually ended following a mishap in the Market Place at Market Lavington, around 1933. When another driver braked very sharply for some reason, he was thrown from where he was standing at the back to the front of the bus and sustained serious leg injuries, spending months in hospital. He was told that he would never walk again, but he did do so, with great tenacity. Harry had married Phyllis (Betty) Pike, daughter of George Pike, a Market Lavington butcher, in April 1932. So Harry and his wife could still have an income after he could no longer drive buses, Betty's father bought them a grocery business in the High Street, opposite Edwin Potter's old house. They were grocers and newsagents until 1969 and Harry even walked round the village delivering papers.

The board was told at the end of 1926 that Fred Sayer had arranged for occupation of part of 21A Market Place in Devizes for use as an office, as a sub-tenant of Mr G. Sheppard. Although this was recorded as not to be pursued, an address of 18 Market Place had replaced 59 Northgate Street in advertisements from June 1926, so the exact circumstances are unclear. In January 1928 there was concern that Sheppard's merchandise was obstructing access for L&D's customers and he was asked to improve matters. At the same time the company requested a rent reduction to £30 per year but this was refused. Also in January 1928, it was proposed that the house in Salisbury acquired with the Hall business should be sold for £750 to Charles Sparrow, who was still the tenant.

It appears that around this time, the first attempts were made at selling the company. BTMC were interested in acquiring it and discussions were held but the price asked was again deemed too high. An approach was also received from Frank Wort (of Wort & Way) of Salisbury. The directors set a price of £24,750, to include thirty-six vehicles, and agreed to meet with Wort and his associates but declined to supply copies of the accounts. Nothing further came from this enquiry. In late 1928, the services of Messrs Williams of Newport, Monmouthshire, were engaged. They were introduction agents who were charged with finding a buyer for the company. However, nothing was heard from them by April 1929 and their failed services were dispensed with at the end of that year. The Great Western Railway also ran bus services in parts of the West Country and officials had visited Market Lavington and 'made certain enquiries', but again, nothing transpired.

Now that 'all-weather' and totally enclosed coaches were available, it was becoming increasingly difficult to make L&D's remaining old-style charabancs attractive to potential private hire customers or to patrons of advertised excursions. Business was no doubt being lost to competitors. In April 1929 it was stated in the board minutes that 'three new all-weather' vehicles had been purchased for £275 each, but this does not match known fleet intake at that time. However, a fourteen-seat Chevrolet (MW 4568) was acquired in May and licensed to F. H. Sayer, so it may have been his property rather than the company's. In the second half of 1929, five single-deck thirty-two-seat rear-entrance Dodson saloon bus bodies were purchased from Wilts & Dorset, who

Posing at Tinhead, near Edington, in 1927 are conductor Stan Weston (believed to be related to Mabel Sayer) and driver Jack Boulton. They could have been operating the Market Lavington–Trowbridge service. Note the L&DMS timetable display board top left. (S. Chislett Collection)

had no further use for them. At least three of these were used to re-body some L&D coaches – AEC YC-type XM 867 and AEC 502s MR 865/3575. In autumn of that year, there was a pressing need to replace the fourteen-seat Crossley charabancs with something more modern. It was agreed in principle to buy two new large bodies and two fourteen or twenty-seat vehicles, total cost not to exceed £1,200, but Sayer could not achieve this within the cost authorised. He then proposed to accept a quotation from Gilford for two chassis at £595 each, with twenty-seat bodies by Heaver at £275 each, in a part exchange for two Crossleys, but this was vetoed by the other directors.

There was also a need to update the image in the excursion advertisements in the press; from the 1930 season, the drawing of an open charabanc was replaced by one of an 'all weather' coach. Trowbridge and Melksham contact telephone numbers began to feature too – these were probably for local booking agents rather than company premises in those towns.

Another, more substantial, net loss was recorded for the year ended September 1929 – £1,413 18s 1d. Probably consequentially, the services of two drivers and a mechanic were dispensed with that autumn. However, the British economy, along with that of all other western industrialised countries, was about to spiral further into a deep ten-year recession, following the collapse of trading on the New York Stock Exchange in October 1929, known as the Wall Street Crash. During the early 1930s, large amounts were wiped off share values, credit was squeezed, businesses closed or were sold and workers were laid off. This did not bode well for L&DMS, or for any other firm seeking to borrow money.

On a more cheerful note, Frederick Sayer Junior got married to Jessica Trotter on 1 May 1929. Jessica, born in 1905 at Lydd in Kent, was the daughter of William Trotter, landlord of the Volunteer Arms in Church Street, who was also a firewood dealer. The Trotters had arrived in Market Lavington by 1911 and just a few years after that would have come into close contact with the Sayers, whose buses were kept in the yard of the Volunteer Arms, possibly until garaging behind Ivydene was available. The local press recorded that an incredible 600–700 people, if the report was correct, gathered in and around St Mary's church in Market Lavington, followed by a reception for forty guests at the Volunteer Arms and the subsequent departure of the couple for a honeymoon in Bournemouth, though probably not on an L&DMS coach trip.

In January 1930, a warning from the bank was received by L&DMS. Their letter stated that they were concerned about the company's low level of funds and required that the overdraft be reduced. In April 1930, funding was found to purchase HR 9881, a Chevrolet fourteen-seat coach from Laurence Alexander of nearby Lydeway, while in June another second-hand AEC Y-type chassis was registered MW 7482 and given a thirty-two-seat coach body, probably also second-hand. Some Lancia vehicles had been offered to the company in part exchange for three Crossleys, and also a 1928 Gilford chassis in part exchange for an old Daimler chassis. Despite their concerns, the bank agreed to advance the money to pay for these, through a separate loan account. Three Lancia Pentaiotas with twenty-seat bus bodywork by Heaver arrived in July 1930 (MW 7726–8), along with a fourteen-seat Chevrolet bus registered XV 6211. The latter originated from H. H. Wolstenholme, trading as Andover & District, and

This staff group was photographed in 1928, with an 'all-weather' open charabanc with side-screens behind them. Left to right: back row – Fred Parfitt, Bill Trotter, Tom Smith and George Sheppard; middle row – Albert Webb and Melville Bailey; front row – Reg Sheppard, Jack Boulton and Reg Potter. (L. Tancock Collection)

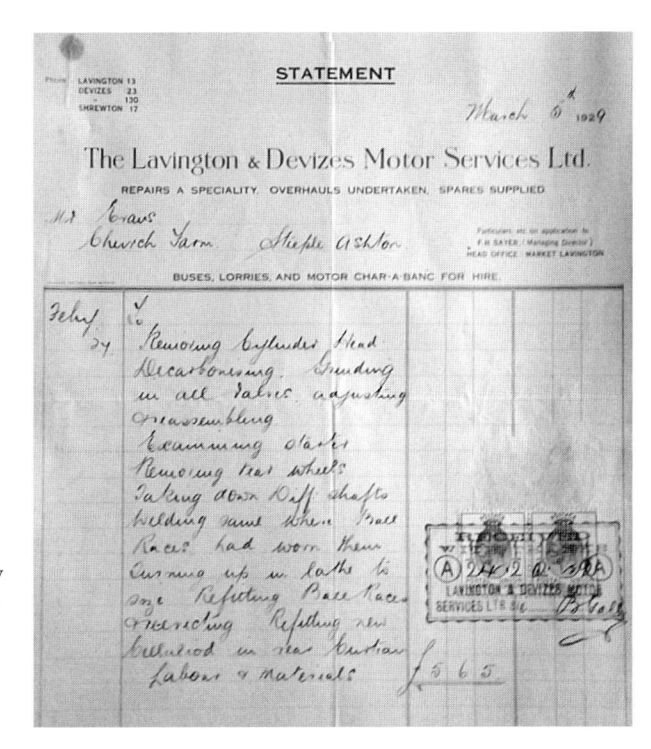

An invoice from 1929, issued by L&DMS for vehicle repairs, has survived. Mr Evans of Church Farm, Steeple Ashton, paid £5 6s 5d for the work detailed. (MLM)

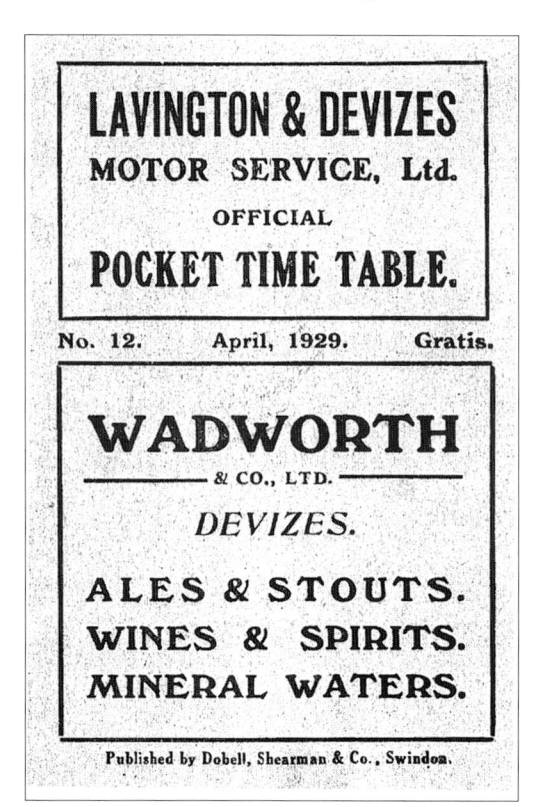

> **LAVINGTON & DEVIZES**
> **MOTOR SERVICE, Ltd.**
> OFFICIAL
> **POCKET TIME TABLE.**
>
> No. 12.   April, 1929.   Gratis.
>
> **WADWORTH**
> & CO., LTD.
> *DEVIZES.*
>
> **ALES & STOUTS.**
> **WINES & SPIRITS.**
> **MINERAL WATERS.**
>
> Published by Dobell, Shearman & Co., Swindon.

L&DMS regularly issued their own little pocket timetable books in conjunction with a commercial publisher and part-funded by advertising for local businesses. This is the cover for the April 1929 edition. (MLM)

> **LAVINGTON & DEVIZES**
> **MOTOR SERVICES, LTD.**
>
> GREEN MOTOR COACHES.
>
> SEATING CAPACITY
> 14, 22, 28 and 32.
> OPEN OR CLOSED.
>
> Private Parties of 14 to 600 Catered For
> With Our Own Fleet.
>
> THE MANAGEMENT WILL BE PLEASED
> TO SUPPLY QUOTATIONS FOR LARGE OR
> SMALL PARTIES FOR SUMMER OUTINGS.
> SPECIAL TERMS FOR SCHOOLS AND
> CLUBS   SATISFACTION GUARANTEED.
>
> For Particulars apply
> HEAD OFFICE,
> MARKET LAVINGTON, WILTS.
> Telephone   Lavington 13.

From the same timetable, this is the advertisement for the private hire facilities offered by L&DMS's Green Motor Coaches. (MLM)

RETURN FARES.
Bath, Box, Melksham, Devizes and Market Lavington Service.

	s.	d.
Bath and Box (Lamb Inn)	1	0
„ Wormwood	1	6
„ Atworth	1	9
„ Shaw Church	2	0
„ Melksham	2	0
„ Seend (New Inn)	3	0
„ Devizes	3	6
„ Lavington	4	6
Box and Seend (New Inn)	3	0
Atworth and Lavington	3	6

	s.	d.
Melksham and Lavington	3	0
„ Devizes	1	6
„ Atworth	1	0
Bath and Erlestoke	4	3
„ Tinhead	4	0
„ Edington	3	9
„ Steeple Ashton	3	9
„ Keevil	3	0
„ Semington	2	6

W. E. CHIVERS & SONS, Ltd.

**Builders & Contractors,
Joinery Manufacturers,
Builders' Merchants,**

Bank & Shop Fittings and Joinery for Housing Schemes
Joinery Supplied to the Trade.

Telephone: Devizes 121 & 122.
Telegrams: "Chivers, Devizes 121." **DEVIZES, Wilts.**

21

Another extract from the 1929 timetable booklet.

was acquired from Wilts & Dorset, who had used it as a baggage van. Another Lancia/Heaver bus (MW 8248) arrived in January 1931.

As the principal of a locally based company, Fred Sayer continued to be active in the community. At the end of 1929, the village fire engine was damaged in an accident and subsequently the Parish Council settled a bill for £3 14s submitted by L&DMS for its repair. In March 1930 it was recorded that the Market Lavington Band was given a magic lantern picture show in the Parish Room, thanks to Fred. Fred Sayer Junior and Harry Hobbs were acknowledged for operating the projection equipment.

In terms of a potential purchase offer for the company, the courtship of the Great Western Railway by directors of L&DMS continued. In early 1930, talks were held but by the spring of that year, the GWR had declared that they were not interested. A final engagement was attempted, with a price tag of £22,000, but a refusal by letter dated 14 August closed the matter. Although the L&D board minutes during 1929 and 1930 refer to contacts with the GWR, it should be noted that there had already been developments regarding the GWR's motor bus services in the West Country. New legislation had allowed mainline railway companies such as the GWR and the Southern Railway to operate or acquire motor bus services. However, what actually happened was that the railway companies decided instead to invest in the major territorial bus companies. From 1 January 1929, two new subsidiary companies took over the operations of National Omnibus & Transport Co. Ltd in the west of England. These were Western National Omnibus Co. Ltd, to run the National services in the GWR's area and to acquire the GWR's own bus services, and the Southern National

In 1929, Fred Sayer junior married Jess Trotter, daughter of William Trotter, the landlord of the Volunteer Arms. We do not have a photograph of Fred junior around that time, but here is one of a young Jess, probably taken by Mr Burgess, the Market Lavington-based professional photographer. By the late 1930s, her sister Ivy had become the licensee of the Volunteer Arms in succession to her father. (MLM)

Considered to have been taken around 1929/1930, this impressive line-up of L&DMS all-weather coaches and charabancs is in Market Lavington marketplace. The seats in the nearest vehicle (an AEC rebuild) look far more comfortable than the ones in the early charabancs. In the background are the remains of the former house seen in the view on page 30, the surviving walls of which have been incorporated into a parking compound for L&DMS vehicles. Visible through the opening are rather antiquated-looking buses. (L. Tancock Collection)

On 12 April 1930, one of the Great Western Railway's excursion trains arrived at Lavington station. The day-trip passengers alighted and transferred to a convoy of L&DMS vehicles for the onward journey to Stonehenge and Old Sarum, across Salisbury Plain. One can identify the three vehicles on the right: at the front is an REO Speedwagon Model F, registered HU 3245; in the middle, one of the AEC rebuilds; and at the rear it looks like XM 867, a former AEC lorry chassis, seemingly now with an Associated Daimler radiator and given an all-weather coach body in 1924. The latter was subsequently re-bodied as a bus, with a Dodson body acquired from Wilts & Dorset and then modified. (MLM)

Omnibus Co. Ltd, to run the services in the Southern Railway's area. Western National was initially owned by National O&T and the GWR on a 50/50 basis. In February 1931, Thomas Tilling Ltd purchased a controlling interest in the parent National O&T and also in the subsidiary companies. Similarly, the financially ailing Wilts & Dorset Motor Services Ltd was purchased on 1 July 1931 by the Southern Railway and Tilling & British Automobile Traction Co. Ltd, without the involvement of the GWR. Bath Electric Tramways Ltd and Bath Tramways Motor Co. Ltd were also not subject to GWR investment, although they remained on good terms with the railway company.

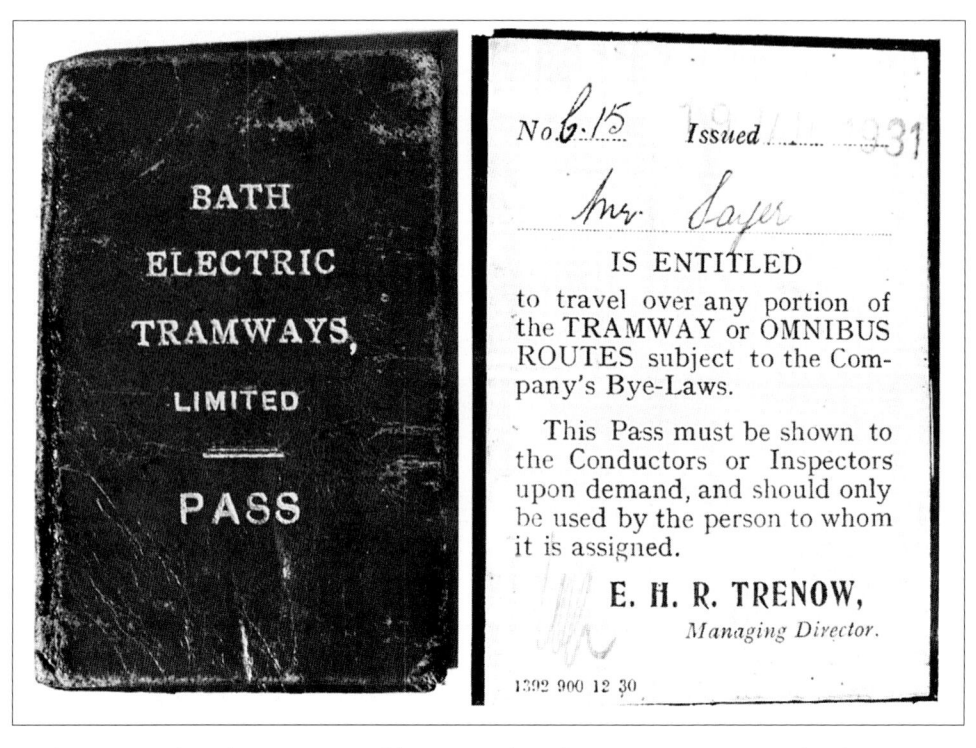

Fred Sayer must have been on reasonable terms with Bath Electric Tramways and Bath Tramways Motor Co., as this pass for free travel, leather bound and bottle green in colour, was issued for him by BET on 19 January 1931; hopefully, Fred reciprocated. (S. Chislett Collection)

Legislation and Consolidation

Since the start of motor bus services, licensing or regulation of vehicles and services was localised and fragmented, especially in rural areas. Although local authorities had powers under the Town Police Clauses Act, as they did for horse-drawn and motor hackney carriages, there was considerable variation in their involvement with buses. By exercising their powers, some attempted to coordinate or limit services, in the interests of reducing traffic congestion in town centres or avoiding wasteful duplication. Only some authorities inspected vehicles for roadworthiness. In some places there was competition between operators on the whole or part of routes – both healthy and unhealthy – although area agreements between the main providers did give some self-regulation. In general, the small village-based carriers and bus operators respected each others' catchment areas or clientele and the inhabitants usually remained loyal to a specific one in cases where there was a choice.

However, a seminal piece of legislation – The Road Traffic Act 1930 – changed all that. It brought coordination and quantity control to the licensing of services, and national requirements for the licensing of drivers, conductors and vehicles; it also introduced regulation of fares. It was administered by a number of area traffic commissioners, who decided what services should run, at what level and by whom. When competing applications were received, they could hold a hearing at a traffic court, where operators could be legally represented to promote and protect their interests and could lodge objections to the plans of others. Having heard all the evidence, the commissioner would then make a decision, and the necessary road service licences (RSLs) would be issued for a set period of time. Until the first hearings for RSLs could be held in the second part of 1931, existing services were allowed to continue under transitional provisions. Most of Wiltshire was placed in the Southern traffic area, but in 1934 there was rationalisation whereby the Southern area was divided up mainly into the enlarged adjoining Western and South Eastern traffic areas.

In 1930, just prior to the enactment of the new legislation, L&DMS could be considered to have been the dominant provider of bus services from Devizes, and had succeeded in keeping the town as a 'frontier', at the extremity of the territory of four major operators who each ran one service into it – Bath Tramways Motor Co., Wilts &

Dorset Motor Services, Western National Omnibus Co. and Bristol Tramways. Wilts & Dorset had only returned to Devizes that year, with a service 21/21A to Salisbury or Andover via Lydeway, Rushall and Upavon. There was a plethora of carriers and smaller operators, whose services mainly ran only on certain days of the week, including E. & C. Sudweeks (Blue Cars) of Devizes, L. N. King & D. R. Jones of Bromham, Lampards Garages of Pewsey, C. J. Bodman of Worton, L. T. Alexander (Queen of the Road) of Lydeway, A. W. Hadrell & Sons of Calne, W. Hamblin of Marlborough, J. Crook & Sons of Melksham, P. J. Card of Devizes and W. C. Mortimer (Upavon & District) of Upavon.

However, on some routes, L&DMS did not have all the traffic to itself, either before or after the introduction of road service licensing. On parts of the Trowbridge services, there was also Sudweeks, who ran regularly from Devizes to Trowbridge via Potterne and Worton, joining the L&D route at Great Cheverell, but also serving Coulston and Keevil. This was granted by the traffic commissioners in spring 1932, despite objections from L&DMS and from Western National. Bodman ran from Devizes to Trowbridge on Tuesdays and Saturdays, via Worton, Erlestoke, Edington and Steeple Ashton. Sudweeks also operated between Devizes, Bromham, Sandy Lane, Calne and Chippenham, while between Devizes and Bromham/Westbrook, there was King & Jones of Overton Garage, Bromham, who concentrated mainly on Thursdays and Saturdays. Lampard's Garages also linked Pewsey to Devizes, albeit via Upavon and Rushall; Card covered All Cannings, Alton Barnes and Horton on Devizes' market day; Alexander ran a service into Devizes from Easterton, Urchfont and Lydeway, but didn't encroach on Market Lavington.

One small local operator who took advantage of the acquisitive policies of Western National to leave the business before the new legislation took effect was Ernest Edwin Piper. He first operated in Surrey from late 1924 to summer 1926, when he returned to his native East Sussex, leaving his business partner Leslie Chell to carry on. He then started the Red Saloon Motor Services, running into Eastbourne in competition with Southdown. Having made a competitive nuisance of himself, he then capitalised by selling his business to Southdown Motor Services. His final stop was Devizes, where he set up his Red Bus concern, running thence to Trowbridge in competition with Western National, as well as in the Melksham area. His somewhat piratical activities included offering cut-price fares and operating unscheduled timings in a quest to poach custom from Western National. Piper was no doubt pleased to be approached by the latter and be offered £3,674 for the purchase of his business in order to get rid of him. However, this was a sensitive area, and Western National had to gain agreement from BTMC, L&DMS and Wilts & Dorset before the takeover could occur on 1 June 1931. That was not quite the last heard of Ernest Piper, as at a meeting between Alfred Chivers and Bert Smith of Western National at 206 Brompton Road in London (National's headquarters), Chivers courteously sought permission to employ Piper. No doubt there were more important matters discussed too – such as Western National's interest in taking over L&DMS!

The first L&DMS applications for road service licences, to continue bus services operated by them in the past year, as well as a good selection of excursions and tours from Market Lavington and Devizes, were published in June 1931. Although shown in an August 1930 L&DMS timetable, the journeys between Bath and Calne may not have been operated by them by then and were not included in the 1931 applications, so it is assumed these were entirely operated by BTMC by mid-1931. However, two services were subject to applications for licences that seem to have started some time after August 1930. One was another route from Market Lavington to Devizes, but via Easterton, Easterton Sands and Potterne, with one round trip on Thursdays and one on Saturday evenings. The other was a service from Tidworth to Andover via Ludgershall, Redenham, Appleshaw and Weyhill, and seems to have been in competition with Wilts & Dorset. It was mentioned in the L&DMS entry in the *Motor Transport Year Book* for 1931/2, but was short-lived. It was some distance away from Market Lavington and well outside the company's normal sphere of operations; a likely vigorous response from Wilts & Dorset, through whose territory it ran, probably hastened its demise, possibly after it was refused an RSL if the traffic commissioners felt its recent introduction had been opportunistic. It could have been introduced as a bargaining point, perhaps in order to encourage Raymond Longman, the manager of Wilts & Dorset, to make an attractive offer for buying the company! The same issue of the year book stated that L&DMS had fifteen buses, twenty coaches and one lorry in its fleet.

During 1931, area agreements were refreshed between the major operators. L&DMS were prepared to sell to either Western National or Wilts & Dorset, especially as there was another loss in 1929/30 of £821 9s 8d. The existence and development of L&DMS ten years earlier had thwarted some ambitions of Wilts & Dorset and National, so they were interested in L&D being for sale. Alfred Chivers had indeed been approached in spring 1931 by Wilts & Dorset and met with Raymond Longman. However, there was still the question of boundary agreements, which would require the L&D operations to be untidily divided. No decision was reached, although negotiations were allowed to remain open.

Fred Sayer had arranged for the acquisition of two second-hand buses in late 1931. These were YV 3926/7, ADC 416A twenty-eight-seat buses with bodies by Hall Lewis, previously owned by Samuelsons of London, SW1. In addition, the 1928 Gilford 168SD chassis was given a second-hand Wycombe twenty-six-seat body from another source and registered WV 521. Their purchase had not been sanctioned by the full board, for which Sayer received a reprimand, and the hire purchase payments for two of them curiously came from an employee – George O'Reilly.

In November 1931, the Great Western Railway decided to sell its 67 per cent holding in the Bristol Tramways & Carriage Co. Ltd, of which it had obtained a controlling interest from Imperial Tramways in 1929, apparently as it belatedly realised that it had no statutory powers to operate trams. The purchaser was the associated Western National, which had its share capital increased to allow the acquisition of £1.053 million worth of preference and ordinary shares. Western National's parent, National Omnibus & Transport, then purchased 320 ordinary shares in BT&CC and passed them to Western National, making BT&CC a subsidiary of Western National. Next, National O&T purchased a number of shares in Bath Electric Tramways Ltd (3,817 5 per cent preference, 2,440 ordinary and 4,906 deferred), which were also transferred

Lavington & Devizes Motor Services

410F — 410M NOTE—LIGHT FIGURES FROM 1201 A.M. TO 1200 NOON HEAVY DARK FIGURES FROM 1201 P.M. TO 1200 MIDNIGHT **410F — 410M**

LAVINGTON & DEVIZES MOTOR SERVICE, LTD.—continued.

410F — MARKET LAVINGTON, URCHFONT AND DEVIZES — 410F

DOWN						UP		
C	SO		SUNS			C		SUNS
730	900	130	720	MARKET LAVINGTON		↑545	345	1045
735	905	135	725	EASTERTON		540	340	1040
740	915	145	735	URCHFONT		530	330	1030
..	925	155	745	BELL INN		..	320	1020
845	945	210	805↓	DEVIZES		430	300	1000

C MONS. TO FRIS. ONLY, AND WILL NOT RUN WHEN DEVIZES SECONDARY SCHOOL IS CLOSED. **SO** SATS. ONLY

410G — MARKET LAVINGTON, DEVIZES AND TROWBRIDGE — 410G

DOWN						DAILY				UP			
	SO		TO		SO		SUNS				TO		TS	SO		SUNS
900	1230	200	..	510	715	130	530	MARKET LAVINGTON	..	130	500	700	1000	1145	400	1000
..	..	..	330	..	..	..	..	DEVIZES	..	1145	..	..	..	..	..	..
..	..	..	345	..	..	..	..	POTTERNE	..	1130	..	..	..	..	..	..
905	1235	205	..	515	720	135	535	LITTLETON PANNELL	..	..	125	455	655	955	1140	355	955
910	1240	210	410	520	725	140	540	GREAT CHEVERELL	..	1105	120	450	650	950	1135	350	950
915	1245	215	415	525	730	145	545	ERLFSTOKE	..	1100	115	445	645	945	1130	345	945
925	1255	225	425	535	740	155	555	TINHEAD	..	1050	105	435	635	935	1120	335	935
930	100	230	430	540	745	200	600	EDINGTON	..	1045	100	430	630	930	1115	330	930
935	105	235	435	545	750	205	605	BRATTON	..	1040	1255	425	625	925	1110	325	925
945	115	245	445	555	800	215	615	STEEPLE ASHTON	..	1030	1245	415	615	915	1100	315	915
955	125	255	455	605	810	225	625	HILDERTON	..	1020	1235	405	605	905	1050	305	905
1000	130	300	500	610	815	230	630↓	TROWBRIDGE	..	1015	1230	400	600	900	1045	300	900

SO SATS. ONLY. **TO** THURS. ONLY. **TS** THURS. AND SATS. ONLY

410H — MARKET LAVINGTON, DEVIZES AND CHIPPENHAM — 410H

DOWN							DAILY	UP				
SO		TX	TO	SO	SO		SUNS			SO	SO		SUNS
830	..	..	..	..	..	130	700	MARKET LAVINGTON	..	↑	..	1045	500	1000
845	..	..	..	..	..	145	720	POTTERNE	..	..	..	1030	440	940
900	900	100	200	500	730	200	730	DEVIZES	..	1130	430	715	1015	430	930
..	905	105	205	505	735	205	735	BACON FACTORY	..	1125	425	710	1010	425	925
..	915	115	215	515	745	215	745	ROWDE	..	1115	415	700	1000	415	915
..	920	120	220	520	750	220	750	BELL INN	..	1110	410	655	955	410	910
..	930	130	230	530	800	230	800	BROMHAM	..	1100	400	645	945	400	900
..	940	140	240	540	810	240	810	SANDY LANE	..	1050	350	635	935	350	850
..	945	145	245	545	815	245	815	DERRY HILL	..	1045	345	630	930	345	845
..	1000	200	300	600	830	300	830↓	CHIPPENHAM	..	1030	330	615	915	330	830

SO SATS. ONLY. **TO** THURS. ONLY. **TX** NOT THURS

410J — CODFORD AND SALISBURY — 410J

DOWN					TUES., SATS. AND SUNS. ONLY	UP			
TUES.	SATS.		SUNS			TUES.	SATS.		SUNS
945	930	500	115	CODFORD	..	↑510	410	1040	1015
955	940	510	125	WYLYE (P.O.)	..	500	400	1030	1005
1005	950	520	130	STEEPLE LANGFORD	..	450	350	1020	1000
1015	1000	530	140	STAPLEFORD	..	440	340	1010	950
1025	1010	540	145	SOUTH NEWTON	..	430	330	955	945
1035	1020	550	150	WILTON	..	420	320	945	940
1055	1040	610	200↓	SALISBURY	..	400	300	930	930

410K — CODFORD AND FROME — 410K

DOWN	WEDNESDAYS ONLY	UP
925	CODFORD	↑450
950	HEYTESBURY	430
1000	WARMINSTER	415
1020	CROCKERTON	400
1035	HORNINGSHAM	335
1050	WEST WOODLANDS	315
1105↓	FROME	300

410L — CODFORD AND DEVIZES — 410L

DOWN	THURSDAYS ONLY	UP
925	CODFORD	↑515
1000	WARMINSTER	440
1030	IMBER	410
1050	MARKET LAVINGTON	350
1120↓	DEVIZES	330

410M — HINDON AND SALISBURY — 410M

DOWN					DAILY	UP			
	SO		SUNS			TX	Tu	SO	SUNS
930	500	430	800	HINDON	..	↑415	515	1045	330	1045
935	505	435	805	FONTHILL BISHOP	..	410	510	1040	325	1040
940	510	440	810	CHILMARK	..	405	505	1030	320	1030
950	520	450	820	TEFFONT MAGNA	..	355	455	1020	310	1020
1000	530	500	830	DINTON	..	345	445	1010	300	1010
1010	540	510	840	BARFORD ST. MARTIN	..	335	435	1000	250	1000
1030	605	530	900	WILTON	..	315	415	945	280	945
1045	615	545	915↓	SALISBURY	..	300	400	930	215	930

SO SATS. ONLY. **Tu** TUES. ONLY. **TX** NOT TUES.

858

L&DMS services 410F–M from the spring 1931 *Roadway* timetable booklet.

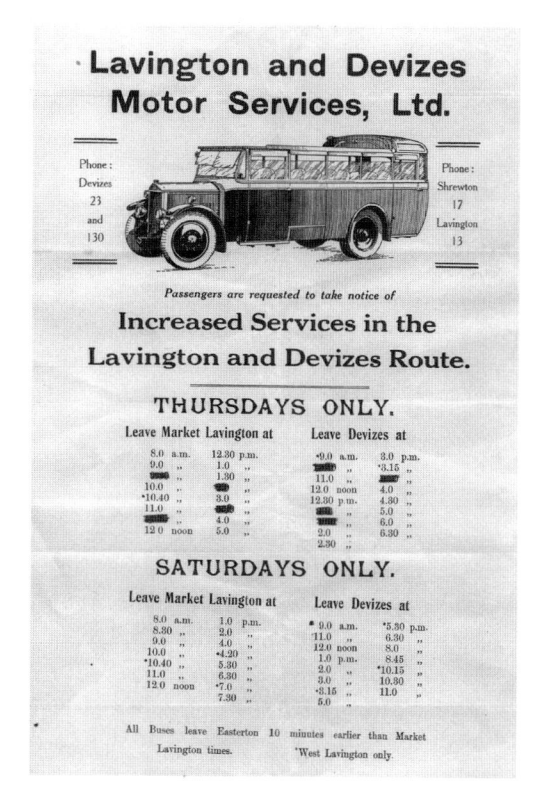

Sometime after the grant of the first road service licences in summer 1931, the Market Lavington–Devizes service was extended to start from Easterton, at least on Thursdays and Saturdays, as evidenced by this undated handbill. (R. Grimley Collection)

to Western National. Meanwhile, the Bath Tramways Motor Co. became owned in equal share by BET and BT&CC.

The 11 March 1932 board meeting of L&DMS, the last recorded when the Chivers brothers and Fred Sayer were in control, was a gloomy affair. The net loss for 1930/1 was £2,261 8s 11d. Fred Sayer had been ill since February 1931 and unable to give matters his full attention; he had not drawn a salary since the end of the previous October. His health had now permitted him to resume his duties but he reported that there had been some friction between himself and other managers – George O'Reilly and Bruce Gale. Wage rates had been cut and men laid off out of season, and it was proposed to withdraw the Hindon–Salisbury service and those starting at Codford, although this did not occur. The arrangement for overnight bus parking at Western National's Trowbridge depot was to cease from 25 March 1932, the vehicle instead being kept for free in a local car park. An advertisement had been placed in *Motor Transport* and *Commercial Motor* magazines for the sale of the business, but there had been no replies. Another attempt to advertise would be made, including in some national and regional newspapers. However, an unnamed party had offered to buy the shares of the three Chivers brothers.

The final vehicle purchased by L&DMS under independent ownership was UM 8861 in March 1932 – another ADC 416A, but with a body by John Taylor of Barnsley, purchased from Hurton of Retford. It originated with Warburton's Bus Service of

A further example of Mabel Sayer's fancy dress costume for Hospital Week – in 1931 she decided to dress up as a schoolgirl. (MLM)

In 1932, Mabel Sayer pretended to be a fortune teller and is seen here in Market Lavington outside Phillips' shop, probably collecting money during the carnival procession. (MLM)

Headingley, near Leeds, in April 1927 and after three months was acquired by West Yorkshire Road Car, who used it until it went to Hurton.

An application was made to the traffic commissioner in spring 1932 to reduce the running times on various services. The times that had been scheduled had been somewhat excessive for a while, being based on the old 12 mph speed limit! It was now possible to reduce journey times, for example by fifteen minutes from Market Lavington to Devizes and thirty minutes throughout to Bath.

Fred Sayer (unclear as to whether Senior or Junior) had a minor brush with the law on 25 April 1932. He was stopped by a police constable for driving a car without a rear-view mirror. When challenged, he replied that he did not know he had to have one and thought it was not necessary on smaller vehicles. Despite offering to put one on straight away, he still ended up being summoned to Devizes Borough Petty Session, where he was fined 5s.

In May 1932, the company whose parent had indirectly spawned the existence of Lavington & Devizes Motor Services, and had been associated with it in various ways, became its owner.

In December 1931, L&DMS acquired two 1928-vintage Associated Daimler (ADC) 416A buses, with bodywork by Hall Lewis. They came from Samuelsons of London, SW1. YV 3926 was caught on film after withdrawal by Bath Tramways Motor Co., shortly before it was scrapped in August 1937. (G. Bruce Collection)

The other Samuelsons ADC 416A (YV 3927) is seen on the London–Oxford–Birmingham express service, before migrating to rural Wiltshire. (G. Bruce Collection)

Under New Ownership

By the time of the next recorded L&DMS board meeting on 21 May 1932, the company's shares and debentures had been acquired in the names of four directors of the Bath Tramways Motor Co. Ltd – Evelyn Henry Raynward Trenow, John Aime Roney, Col. Hugh Clutterbuck and Maj. Eric Long. Trenow and Roney were appointed directors, in place of Fred Sayers and the Chivers brothers, who all resigned. The first entry in a new L&DMS accounts ledger is for 22 May, so operational control of L&DMS seems to have effectively passed to BTMC by then, although the new acquisition was kept as a separate subsidiary company, to avoid having to renegotiate the boundary agreements with adjoining operators.

These developments came as something of a traumatic disappointment to Western National and Wilts & Dorset, but they only had themselves to blame, as they had lost out due to their previous indecisiveness when given the opportunity to purchase L&DMS, and should never have let the situation occur. However, the sale to BTMC avoided the difficulties of dividing the business between them and the need to change their sensitive boundary agreements. Of some bearing was the fact that BTMC was not associated with one of the railway companies. Although Wilts & Dorset was unable to consolidate the western side of its territory, at least Western National had some comfort inasmuch as it, at that time, was effectively the owner of the Bristol Tramways & Carriage Co., which had a substantial holding in BTMC!

It may now be worth summarising the operations and vehicles of L&DMS at the time that control passed to BTMC. The stage services were:

Easterton/Market Lavington–Potterne–Devizes (daily)
Market Lavington–Easterton–Urchfont–Devizes (Sunday)
Pewsey–Woodborough–All Cannings–Devizes (Tuesday, Thursday and Saturday)
Market Lavington–Potterne–Devizes–Melksham–Box–Bath (daily)
Market Lavington–Great Cheverell–Erlestoke–Steeple Ashton–Trowbridge (daily)
Trowbridge–Steeple Ashton–Erlestoke–Great Cheverell–Potterne–Devizes (Thursday)
Market Lavington–Erlestoke–Steeple Ashton–Melksham–Box–Bath (Wednesday and Saturday)

A newspaper advertisement for excursions offered in June 1932, just after control of L&DMS passed to Bath Tramways Motor Co. (MLM)

Market Lavington–Potterne–Devizes–Bromham–Derry Hill–Chippenham (daily)
Devizes–Potterne–West Lavington–Shrewton–Stapleford–Wilton–Salisbury (daily), with some journeys running Orcheston–Salisbury
Hindon–Chilmark–Dinton–Wilton–Salisbury (daily)
Codford–Wylye–Stapleford–Wilton–Salisbury (Tuesday, Saturday and Sunday)
Codford–Warminster–Horningsham–Frome (Wednesday)
Codford–Warminster–Imber–West Lavington–Potterne–Devizes (Thursday)
Market Lavington–Easterton–Urchfont–Chirton–All Cannings–Devizes (schooldays)
Market Lavington–Easterton–Easterton Sands–Potterne–Devizes (Thursday and Saturday)

For the time being, all the services continued unaltered and still unnumbered.

There was also an extensive selection of excursions advertised from Market Lavington and Devizes. For example, in the week commencing Sunday 12 June 1932, the offering was Bournemouth (in addition to the regular summer Tuesday and Friday trip to that town), Longleat (twice), Cheddar and Weston-super-Mare, a lengthy trip to the very popular Aldershot Military Tattoo and a circular tour to Bristol Zoo. Compared with the prices in 1924, by 1932 the costs were reduced considerably, although the period return to Bournemouth remained at 10s 6d.

Around twenty vehicles (thirteen buses and six coaches has been quoted) are thought to have passed into BTMC control, and these are identified on the fleet list in Appendix

2. However, the entry in *Motor Transport Year Book* 1931/2 (if it can be relied on) gave a fleet strength of thirty-five buses and coaches. That total might have included some vehicles no longer in stock by the time of the takeover, and it may be that some further vehicles (for which we have no withdrawal dates) were still owned and possibly also passed to BTMC control, albeit soon disposed of.

There were also several management personnel changes, the most significant of which was the departure of the Sayer family. BTMC issued a £25 cheque to Fred Sayer to cover outstanding wages for the month of May 1932, but the new directors recorded that they were unable to continue to offer him a position 'due to the high expected cost to recondition the fleet'. However, he remained on the payroll for a little longer, and the Sayer family was allowed to remain at Ivydene for a short time, before moving in September 1932 to Woodlands, a bungalow on the Westbury road near Great Cheverell. Fred Sayer Junior continued for a time to drive for the new owners. In the Second World War, he was in the Royal Electrical and Mechanical Engineers (REME). Company secretary Edmund Bull had resigned and was replaced by BET's/BTMC's long-standing secretary, Harry J. Almond. George O'Reilly decided to leave the company, and became a poultry farmer at Cherry Lodge, Common Road, Market

Shortly after they gained control, BTMC acquired two AEC 426 buses for L&DMS. They were new to the General Motor & Carrying Co. Ltd of Kirkcaldy, and then passed to W. Alexander & Son of Falkirk. FG 4886 was withdrawn by BTMC in 1937 and ended up as a farm shed after use by the War Department. (R. F. Mack)

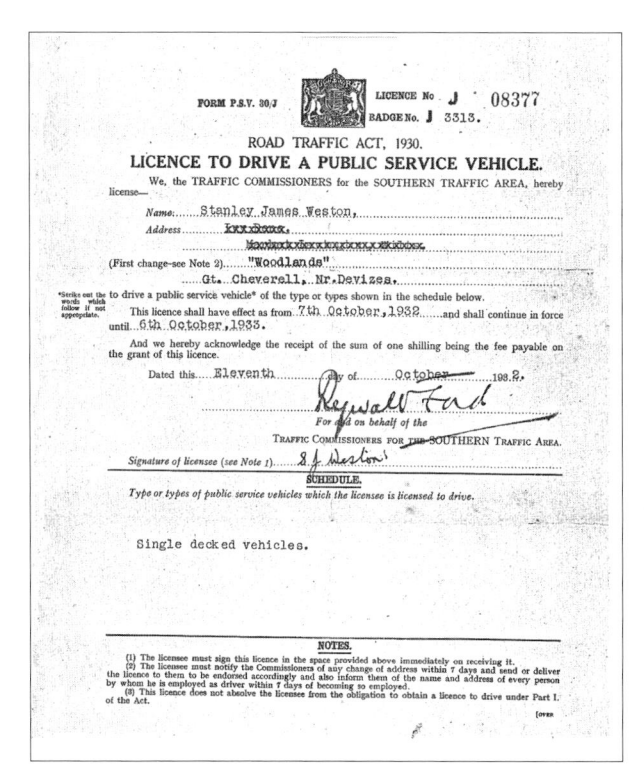

Stan Weston's public service vehicle driver's licence, issued by the traffic commissioners for the Southern traffic area. It is thought that Stan was related to Mabel Sayer (née Weston). An address of Ivydene, Market Lavington, has been deleted, and Woodlands, Great Cheverell, substituted. It is possible that Stan lodged with Fred and Mabel, moved with them to Great Cheverell in 1932 and then drove for Fred's new Beckington Coaches venture. He was still driving buses into the 1980s. (S. Chislett Collection)

Lavington. He passed away in 1948, aged seventy-two, and it is recorded that Harry Chivers sent apologies for being unable to attend the funeral.

John Roney became BTMC's director, responsible for Lavington & Devizes Motor Services. Edward Bruce Gale became the office manager, and by April 1933 the Gale family had become the occupiers of Ivydene. Bruce Gale's son, Michael, recalls that Ivydene was a large property that had a long garden, and at the back was the bus garage and workshop. He remembers watching his father and another employee pushing a measuring wheel device along the roads marked on large maps. They were calculating the mileage for a private hire quotation. To put such charges into context, in 1933 the daily quoted charge for a coach to Bournemouth or Weston-super-Mare was £4 10s for a twenty-seat all-weather coach, £6 for twenty-eight seats and £6 6s for a thirty-two-seat vehicle with glass side screens and a hood.

Michael Gale recalls an amusing anecdote from his childhood years at Ivydene. At the bottom of the garden was the main road through Market Lavington, separated by a wall. Opposite was Potter's farm, and one of Edwin junior's sons said to Michael that if he fetched a jug and one penny, he could have a pint of pigeon's milk. Theresa Gale, Michael's mother, played along with this and he duly went home with some pigeon's milk!

The new owners of L&DMS lost little time in investing to try and restore the business's fortunes – it seems this was greatly needed! From 20 June 1932, board meetings took place at BTMC's registered office in London, EC2, and the first one at

In 1932/3, L&DMS acquired three twenty-seat Commer Invader vehicles – the last arrivals to be licensed to the company. This is thought to be one of them with a double-decker of Wilts & Dorset Motor Services in the background. (L. Tancock Collection)

the new location considered the merits of moving the garage to Devizes from Market Lavington. However, the reroofing and reconditioning of the existing garages was considered, along with an extension, but eventually it was decided not to proceed. In autumn 1932 it was agreed to vacate the Orcheston premises at an early date. Through that summer, BTMC was injecting funding into L&DMS, including for the purchase of additional vehicles to replace the more antiquated Crossley and AEC specimens. By July, two AEC 426 buses had arrived, previously owned by the large Scottish firm of W. Alexander of Falkirk. Both of thirty-two seats, they were registered FG 4422/4886 and had been new to the General Motor & Carrying Co. of Kirkcaldy, Fife. Two further AEC 426s with thirty-two-seat bus bodies by Hall Lewis from the main BTMC fleet, registered FB 7211/12, were stationed at Market Lavington.

In June 1932, BTMC managed to obtain ten AEC 414 buses that had formerly been with Plymouth City Transport. They acquired them from a dealer, W. R. Wintour of London, for the bargain basement price of £30 each, together with the trading in of ten old AEC chassis. In addition, BTMC paid £65 to Plymouth City Transport for spares for these vehicles. They were eventually divided between BTMC and L&DMS, with DR 719/1215 being allocated to Market Lavington in August/September 1932. They were supplemented by two 1930-vintage Commer Invader twenty-seat buses (RG 1316/1411, costing £400 and £300 respectively), which arrived in the September, having previously been owned by River Dee Coaches of Aberdeen.

This timetable from November 1932 confirms that by then the Market Lavington–Potterne–Devizes bus service was starting from Easterton on a daily basis. (R. Grimley Collection)

On 31 October 1932, a special meeting of the board of L&DMS formally approved the transfer of £9,000 of debenture stock from the former directors to the BTMC nominees. By that autumn, at least by 28 November, the main bus service from Market Lavington to Devizes was extended to start at Easterton on a daily basis; this was seemingly approved by the traffic commissioner, despite the less frequent link to town provided from Easterton via Urchfont and Lydeway by L. T. Alexander. The Wednesday and Saturday Market Lavington–Bath via Erlestoke service had been diverted via Great Cheverell, and had gained an afternoon short-working from Bath to Keevil and back, worked during layover time in the city.

The company's Devizes office and agency arrangements were moved to 49 Northgate Street, the premises of Charles Edward Figgins, a hairdresser of long standing. Advertisements for coach excursions had not appeared in the local press in the first part of the 1932 season but were resumed by the new management towards the end of June.

When Fred Sayer moved to Great Cheverell, he took fourteen-seat Chevrolet coach MW 4568 and Reo HU 3245 with him; the former at least appears to have been his personal property. Possibly using some of the money he received for the sale of his L&DMS shares, he established a small garage and coaching operation at Great Cheverell, carrying out private hire. Sayer purchased the goodwill of the passenger transport side of Lodge & Co., who were also haulage contractors, from Beckington near Frome. He perpetuated the trading name of Beckington Coaches. Further vehicles

Lavington and Devizes Motor Services, Limited.

Devizes, Bishops Cannings, Woodborough, Woodbridge Inn, Pewsey.

WEEK-DAY SERVICE.   **SUNDAY SERVICE.**

		D. a.m.	T.&S. a.m.	D. p.m.	T.&S. p.m.	D. p.m.	X. p.m.	p.m.	p.m.
DEVIZES—Market Place	Dep.	9.15	9.45	12.15	3.0	4.30	8.30	2.40	7.15
Bishops Cannings	...	9.25	9.55	12.25	3.10	4.40	8.40	2.50	7.25
Horton	...	9.30	10.0	12.30	3.15	4.45	8.45	2.55	7.30
Allington	...	9.35	10.5	12.35	3.20	4.50	8.50	3.0	7.35
All Cannings	...	9.40	10.10	12.40	3.25	4.55	8.55	3.5	7.40
Stanton	...	9.50	10.20	12.50	3.35	5.5	9.5	3.15	7.50
Alton	...	9.53	10.23	12.53	3.38	5.8	9.8	3.18	7.53
Woodborough	...	9.58	10.28	12.58	3.43	5.13	9.13	3.23	7.58
Bottlesford P.O.	...	10.0	10.30	1.0	3.45	5.15	9.15	3.25	8.0
North Newnton	...	10.5	10.35	1.5	3.50	5.20	9.20	3.30	8.5
Woodbridge Inn	...	10.10	10.40	1.10	3.55	5.25	9.25	3.35	8.10
Manningford	...		10.45		4.0			3.40	8.15
PEWSEY—The Monument	Arr.		10.50		4.5			3.45	8.20

		D. a.m.	T.&S. a.m.	D. p.m.	T.&S. p.m.	D. p.m.		p.m.	p.m.
PEWSEY—The Monument	Dep.		11.0		4.10			4.0	8.30
Manningford	...		11.5		4.15			4.5	8.35
Woodbridge Inn	...	10.10	11.10	1.10	4.20	5.25		4.10	8.40
North Newnton	...	10.15	11.15	1.15	4.25	5.30		4.15	8.45
Bottlesford P.O.	...	10.20	11.20	1.20	4.30	5.35		4.20	8.50
Woodborough	...	10.23	11.22	1.22	4.32	5.37		4.22	8.52
Alton	...	10.27	11.27	1.27	4.37	5.42		4.27	8.57
Stanton	...	10.30	11.30	1.30	4.40	5.45		4.30	9.0
All Cannings	...	10.40	11.40	1.40	4.50	5.55		4.40	9.10
Allington	...	10.45	11.45	1.45	4.55	6.0		4.45	9.15
Horton	...	10.50	11.50	1.50	5.0	6.5		4.50	9.20
Bishops Cannings	...	10.55	11.55	1.55	5.5	6.10		4.55	9.25
DEVIZES—Market Place	Arr.	11.5	12.5	2.5	5.15	6.20		5.5	9.35

D.—Daily.   T.&S.—Thursdays and Saturdays.   X.— Saturdays.

Devizes and Pewsey Fare Table.

                                                                                                      To or From Devizes Pewsey

DEVIZES	...										
Bishops Cann'gs	...	4d.								—	2s. 6d.
Horton	...	5d.	2d.							6d.	2s. 0d.
Allington	...	7d.	5d.	3d.						8d.	2s. 0d.
All Cannings	...	10d.	7d.	6d.	3d.					10d.	1s. 9d.
Alton	...	1s 1d.	10d.	9d.	6d.	3d.				1s. 0d.	1s. 8d.
Woodborough	...	1s. 1d.	1s. 0d	10d.	7d.	5d.	2d.			1s. 3d.	1s. 6d.
Bottlesford	...	1s. 1d.	1s. 0d.	11d.	8d.	6d.	4d.	2d.		1s. 6d.	1s. 3d.
North Newnton	...	1s. 2d.	1s. 1d.	1s. 0d.	9d.	7d.	5d.	4d.	3d.	1s. 6d.	1s. 0d.
Woodbridge Inn	...	1s. 2d.	1s. 1d.	1s. 1d.	10d.	8d.	6d.	5d.	4d.	2d.	1s. 9d.	9d.
Manningford	...	1s. 3d.	1s. 2d.	1s. 2d.	1s. 1d.	11d.	7d.	6d.	5d.	4d.	3d.	2s. 0d.
PEWSEY	...	1s. 6d.	1s. 4d.	1s. 3d.	1s. 2d.	1s. 1d.	10d.	9d.	7d.	7d.	6d.	3d.	2s. 6d.

Woodward, Printer, Devizes.   9—3—33.

A timetable dated 9 March 1933 shows that the Pewsey service was running daily from Devizes as far as Woodbridge Inn.

were acquired: YB 2638, a Lancia that came with the Lodge business, and DK 5826, a thirty-one-seat Gilford 166OT coach acquired from Crew of Bristol, but new to Yelloway of Rochdale. In due course, Fred junior was involved too, as his father's health deteriorated.

Operationally, the Bath–Devizes and Devizes–Salisbury services were combined from 9 January 1933. Some buses worked through from Bath to Salisbury, but the services continued to be advertised separately at that stage. A revised timetable was introduced; on weekdays there were four or five journeys throughout, and three on Sundays, together with various short-workings, such as Bath–Melksham, Melksham–Devizes and Orcheston–Salisbury. The only journeys serving Market Lavington were effectively those starting or finishing at the garage. Licensing remained divided between L&DMS and BTMC, with the latter's journeys losing their 13 designation. However, the majority of the service saw a modernisation in the rolling stock as BTMC's light-blue-liveried 1931 forward entrance Park Royal-bodied AEC Regal buses (FB 9221–6) were then used, running 'on hire' to L&DMS when covering journeys or sections of route that were licensed to the latter. Some of these were allocated to Market Lavington; the remainder worked from Bath.

By 9 March 1933, the Pewsey–Devizes service was altered, inasmuch as the Pewsey–Woodbridge Inn section remained running only on Thursdays, Saturdays and Sundays, but the frequency on the section from Woodbridge Inn to Devizes was increased so that buses ran daily, being diverted between Horton and Devizes via Bishops Cannings. The last vehicle to arrive and be licensed to L&DMS was VT 6172 in April 1933. This was another Commer Invader, this time with a twenty-seat coach body, purchased for £350 after use by Buckley & Cookson of Basford, Staffordshire. However, a further two ex-Plymouth AEC 414s (DR 1217/20) may have been 'purchased' by L&DMS from BTMC in September 1933, although they may have been used by L&D for at least a year previously.

Although L&DMS held licences for a wide range of day excursion destinations, there was a refusal by the Southern area traffic commissioner to grant one for Stonehenge and Old Sarum from Lavington station, in conjunction with the long-standing special trains run by the Great Western Railway. The latter made an inclusive charge for the train fare, coach transfer and admission to Stonehenge, but the part of the fare for the coach transfer of 4s 6d was subject to separate tickets, for which L&DMS made a retrospective claim to the GWR for payment. The traffic commissioner held that the GWR should hold the road service licence, and refused to grant one to L&D. However, this decision was overturned on appeal, by the Minister of Transport, in April 1933, because it was decided that, as L&D was required to take responsibility for the passengers, they should hold the licence.

By the 1930s, girls attending local village schools were sometimes required to attend domestic subjects centres, which usually covered an area. This brought regular business for L&D's bus services, with contracts with Wiltshire County Council to offer return tickets at set fares. In July 1933, arrangements were put in hand for eighteen girls from each of West Lavington and Market Lavington schools to attend Devizes secondary school as a group, once a fortnight for each school, at a return fare of 6d. In September

1934, a similar arrangement applied from Shaw school to Melksham at a return fare of 2*d*, with notice being given to the previous transport contractor – Stringer & Co. of Melksham. Finally, from January 1936 it was decided that, as Mr E. F. Scott of Tilshead had terminated his contract, in future L&D would convey girls once a week from Tilshead school to Shrewton domestic subjects centre on the bus service at a return fare of 6*d*.

The report of the directors to the ordinary general meeting of shareholders of BTMC on 11 July 1933 stated that, in respect of the acquisition of L&DMS, 'a drastic overhaul in all departments was found necessary and it is expected that after the transition period is past, improved working results will be shown'. The 1934 meeting was told that 'the L&D operation has continued at a loss', 'a considerable improvement' a year later and 'a small profit' for the year ending March 1936. BTMC investment in L&DMS had included £45 for a safe at Ivydene in September 1932 and a £500 loan advance in November that year.

An application was made in December 1933 to run excursions from Hindon to Tidworth Tattoo, Shaftesbury Carnival and Hindon Carnival, as well as on other special occasions. However, an objection was forthcoming from Walter Swadling (Victor Motor Services), who was already licensed to run excursions from the Hindon area, thus the L&D application was refused. However, L&D was to be successful in its quest to offer a programme of day trips from Shrewton and other places such as Winterbourne Stoke and Berwick St James, mainly to coastal destinations and also from Codford to Tidworth Tattoo. At that time, military tattoos were very popular, bringing in many coaches from a wide area.

From June 1932, some of the L&D vehicles had their ownership transferred to BTMC. This process was accelerated in January 1934 when ADCs MR 9504, YV 3926/7, UM 8861 and AECs FG 4422, DR 719/1215/17/20 were thus transferred.

The board had decided to dispose of the house owned by the company in Salisbury at 2 Nelson Road, where Charles Sparrow was still in residence at a monthly rent of £2 10*s*. They fixed the sale price as £750, but in February 1934 accepted Sparrow's lower offer of £440.

On 30 April 1934, L&DMS's founder and principal, Frederick Sayer, passed away at home, at the relatively young age of fifty-three. He was buried on 3 May at Locksbrook cemetery in Bath, in the same grave as his father. Mabel, his widow, seems to have carried on with the coach business at Great Cheverell, as the vehicles were listed as licensed to her in 1934, but it is not thought that operations continued for much more than a year. When Sayer's death was recorded in the local press, comment was made about his generosity to the local community. He had presented a trailer fire tender to Market Lavington, which was subsequently put on a motorised chassis in the mid-1930s. He was closely associated with Market Lavington Prize Band, and at one time was an honorary member of the Market Lavington & Easterton Institute. Recognition was made of his work for the local hospital committee's charity events and his similar support also for the Devizes and District hospital committee. Under new ownership, the L&DMS company had continued to be involved with the local fire service, as in October 1932, the parish council noted that Bath Electric Tramways (sic) had offered to keep a motor vehicle to pull the Market Lavington fire pump when the need arose.

From sometime in 1935, the Hindon–Salisbury service had one round trip on Tuesdays extended so as to run from/to Chicklade. This service had always been something of an outlier in the L&D network, having come with the more strategically important Devizes–Salisbury service from the Hall business. Even after the Road Traffic Act, there was considerable competition along the route. Ralph Cox (Wincanton Motor Services) ran on Tuesdays from Wincanton to Salisbury via Mere, Hindon and Dinton, before selling out to Southern National from 1 November 1932, who gave the service the number 50. The latter withdrew as early as the end of April 1934. Three Counties Motors Ltd of Bourton provided three return trips on Saturdays from Bourton, via Mere, East Knoyle and Hindon from around 1929 to 1934, when the firm entered insolvency. Richard Bartlett from East Knoyle ran thence to Salisbury via Hindon on Tuesdays and Thursdays until he sold his bus services to Wilts & Dorset on 21 August 1936. Meanwhile, Walter Swadling (Victor Motor Services) of Tisbury, mentioned earlier, ran Hindon–Tisbury–Salisbury (daily) and East Knoyle–Hindon–Dinton–Salisbury (daily except Wednesdays) until he too sold to Wilts & Dorset – on 5 March 1936. These transactions made W&D the major player on the route. Finally, Fred and Reg Viney (Viney's Motor Service) continued to run from Chilmark to Salisbury via Dinton (weekdays) until they were acquired by H. L. Barber's Skylark Motor Services just after the Second World War. Interestingly, one of Viney's drivers was Jack Hall of the Orcheston clan – a link with the past.

From 11 October 1934, some journeys on the main Easterton–Devizes service were diverted at West Lavington crossroads, to better serve the village by following the route of the Salisbury service down to a place known as The Gun, where they turned round at the junction of the A360 and Rutts Lane. The Gun was actually an old canon that stood on a triangle of grass outside Dial House; although there was local discussion in autumn 1932 about the benefits of removing The Gun, apparently it was eventually a victim of the scrap metal salvage drive in the Second World War. From around late 1933, most journeys on the Chippenham service were curtailed to start from Devizes, only running through from/to Market Lavington principally on alternate Fridays (Great Market days) and Sundays.

The *Motor Transport Year Book* for 1935/6 gives the L&D fleet as being thirteen buses, six coaches and a Fiat touring car. It would appear from the number of coaches given that such activities had been somewhat scaled down, although in June 1935, trips were offered to destinations such as Bristol, Southampton, the Wye Valley, Weston-super-Mare, Wookey Hole, Weymouth, Southsea, Longleat, Swanage and Savernake Forest, as well as the perennial Bournemouth and Aldershot Tattoo. Trips were offered to Epsom racecourse for the Derby and to Ascot races for the Royal Hunt Cup. Day trips to places a considerable distance away had of course become more practicable since the days of the primitive charabancs, due to better roads, higher permitted speeds and great advances in vehicle design, such as fully enclosed bodies and pneumatic tyres. The Wye Valley in Herefordshire was one of the further-away places listed on the licence, and carried the highest fare – 10s 6d.

A sample of the cover used for the combined BTMC and L&DMS timetable booklet, before the latter company was wound up in 1937.

As explained earlier, the existence of L&D's Devizes–Salisbury service was a matter of irritation for Wilts & Dorset, who had let the opportunity pass to conquer that road. In Salisbury, that service and the others under BTMC control continued to terminate at New Canal, a point used by a number of independent operators. Subsequently the Devizes service used the Salt Lane car park and had to stay there even after Wilts & Dorset opened the new Endless Street bus station in 1939. It was therefore not surprising to learn that in November 1935, an approach had been made by both Wilts & Dorset and by Fred & Reg Viney of Chilmark, registering their interest in acquiring the Devizes–Salisbury service. This seems to have been ignored by L&DMS.

The year 1936 saw little overall change, although some alterations were made to the L&D stage carriage services. Around January, the Codford–Frome Wednesday service was diverted to serve Longbridge Deverill between Crockerton and Horningsham. By May, the Pewsey–Devizes service had been reduced again to run on Thursdays, Saturdays and Sundays throughout, while by July that year the following had occurred:

Market Lavington–Urchfont–Devizes (Sundays): also ran Monday–Saturday late afternoon/evening

Market Lavington–Devizes–Chippenham: all journeys advertised on timetables as starting at Devizes

Market Lavington–Easterton Sands–Devizes (Thursdays and Saturday evenings): Saturday journeys replaced by extension of journeys to Easterton Sands on the main Devizes–Easterton service

On 16 April 1936, the services of Laurence Alexander of Lydeway were acquired by Wilts & Dorset for a consideration of £1,000. These were reorganised and numbered as 32 Easterton–Urchfont–Lydeway–Devizes (Mondays–Saturdays) and 33 Beechingstoke–Marden–Chirton–Patney–All Cannings–Etchilhampton–Devizes (Tuesday, Thursday, Saturday and Sunday). Alexander's Excursions & Tours licence was, however, sold to P. J. Card of Devizes. At around the same time, L&DMS considered the purchase of the Blue Cars services of Sudweeks of Devizes, but the matter was left in abeyance.

Submersion into the Tilling Group

A major development occurred in December 1936, when the Bristol Tramways & Carriage Co. Ltd obtained control of Bath Electric Tramways Ltd and its subsidiaries Bath Tramways Motor Co. Ltd and Lavington & Devizes Motor Services Ltd. This was facilitated by an authorised increase in BT&CC share capital of £200,000 worth of ordinary £1 shares on 30 November 1936 and used to acquire 96 per cent of the share capital of BET. The three companies in the 'Bath' group then became effectively subsidiaries of the Bristol company, although for the time being, they retained some autonomy. In the same month, the combined Bath and Lavington fleets were numbered into the series used by Bristol, and the remaining vehicles licensed to L&DMS were transferred to BTMC, presumably being operated 'on hire' when on L&D services or excursions. Vehicles once owned by L&D surviving at that time were (with their new fleet numbers):

AEC YC: XM 867 (873)
AEC 502: MR 865/3575 (874–875)
AEC 414: DR 719/1215/17/20 (801–803/800)
AEC 426: FG 4432/4886 (825–826)
ADC 416A: YV 3926/7, MR 9504, UM 8861 (813–816)
Gilford 168SD: WV 521 (872)
Commer Invader: RG 1316/1411, VT 6172 (869–871)

At the L&DMS board meeting in London on 23 February 1937, it was noted that Major Francis Chapple of Bristol Tramways & Carriage Co. had joined as a director. Chapple, and also John Frederick Heaton of the Tilling Group, had previously joined the board of BET/BTMC. Signifying the beginning of the end, it was proposed to liquidate L&DMS, as its separate existence really no longer had any purpose and corporate matters could be tidied up. However, although there were links between BTMC and Wilts & Dorset through Tilling entity shareholdings, it was not until September 1942 that the two companies came within the same financial group, with the break-up of the Tilling & British Automobile Traction Co. Ltd and the acquisition of W&D by Tilling Motor Services Ltd. Thus, territorial boundary matters continued to be on the agenda for a while longer.

So it was, on 31 March 1937, that an extraordinary general meeting was called, and a special resolution signed by chairman Evelyn Trenow was passed: 'That Lavington & Devizes Motor Services Ltd be wound up voluntarily and that Mr Ernest George Kingston of 1–3 St Augustine's Place, Bristol is hereby appointed liquidator for the purposes of such winding up.' The Bristol address was the headquarters of BT&CC and was also the Registered Office of BET and BTMC from 12 June 1937. In April that year all the L&DMS road service licences for stage carriages and excursions and tours were applied for by BTMC without modification, and subsequently granted. The winding-up formalities had been completed by July 1937, and the ownership of the Market Lavington premises had been conveyed to BTMC.

An application had been made under the L&D name in May 1937 to vary the licence for the Codford–Devizes service, whereby additional journeys would be provided on weekdays from Bugley via Warminster to Oxendean Farm barracks. However, this plan had to be withdrawn due to an objection from Claude S. White of Crockerton.

While these funeral rites were being performed, the Tilling organisation was progressing the purchase of two of the operators of stage carriage services from Devizes, which, perhaps because of no railway influence in BTMC, might otherwise have more naturally passed to Western National. Little progress had previously been made in that respect due to territorial boundary sensitivities, but now the mighty Tilling group was keen to remove some of these small concerns because of the difficulty in obtaining permission from the traffic commissioners for service changes, due to the many competing licence applications. In early 1936 a meeting had considered the best way of placing certain licences deemed inappropriate for acquisition – the excursions of Alexander perhaps being an example. It was agreed that BTMC would purchase the operations of Sudweeks' Blue Cars and seven vehicles for £4,000, and those of L. N. King & D. R. Jones of Bromham with three vehicles for £2,825. It is thought that these purchases were completed in August 1937 and for the time being, the stage services continued separately and unaltered.

When London Transport was absorbing many of the small independent operators in its Country territory, it waited a while before introducing area-based schemes designed to rationalise and coordinate services, encompassing those taken over. The Tilling group did something similar in the Devizes area in respect of Bath Tramways Motor's inherited services when it applied in August 1937 for new and amended stage carriage road service licences, which were to be more Devizes-focused than before. Market Lavington itself was left with just its local service to Devizes. Despite links through Tilling connections, Wilts & Dorset still found it necessary to object to the BTMC application for a new licence for the Bath–Devizes–Salisbury service, without the offer of reciprocal arrangements for W&D. Regardless of the objection, the BTMC applications were granted on 4 November at a hearing held in the home town of their parent company – Bristol! There may well have then been some appeasement negotiations, with BTMC withdrawing from certain areas in favour of W&D,

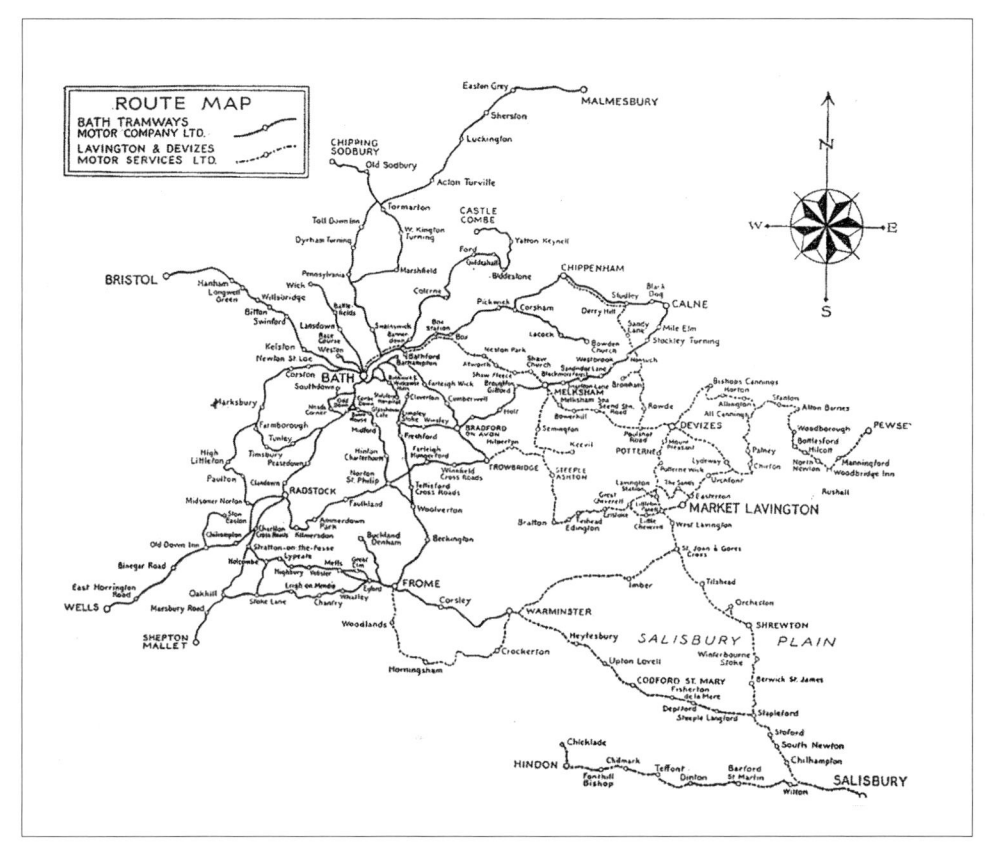

The bus services of the Bath Tramways empire, just before L&DMS was wound up and some services were transferred to Wilts & Dorset or withdrawn.

Bath Tramways Motor Co. took delivery in June 1938 of three AEC Regal coaches with thirty-two-seat Weymann bodies. Numbered 2247–9 and registered GL 5831–3, they were used on the Bath–Devizes and Devizes–Salisbury services. Looking very smart, this is 2247. (J. Batten Collection)

including the transfer of the Hindon service and the Urchfont Sunday journeys for a consideration of £500. The new BTMC licence applications, designed to incorporate some of the former L&D services as well as those of Sudweeks and King & Jones were (with their reference numbers):

H6024: Bath–Box–Wormwood–Atworth–Melksham–Devizes–West Lavington–Shrewton–Salisbury (daily), and H6025: Bath–Box–Corsham–Neston–Atworth, then as H6024 to Salisbury (daily). These two licences combined to provide a Bath–Salisbury link every two hours, with two journeys each way diverted via Orcheston on weekdays. They replaced the former L&D licences H2961 (Devizes–Bath), H4042 (Devizes–Salisbury) and former BTMC licences H278 and 5483 (Bath–Melksham/Devizes).

H6026: Devizes–Rowde–Hawkstreet–Bromham–Westbrook (Thursdays/Saturdays) with one journey each way extended to/from Calne. H6027: Devizes–Rowde–Bromham–Sandy Lane–Derry Hill–Chippenham (daily), and H6028: Devizes–Rowde–Bromham–Sandy Lane–Calne–East Tytherton–Chippenham (daily). They replaced former L&D licence H4041 (Devizes–Chippenham), Sudweeks licence H3994 (Devizes–Chippenham) and King & Jones licences H3813, 4028 & 4029 (Devizes–Bromham/Sandridge/Washbrook).

H6029: Devizes–Potterne–Great Cheverell–Erlestoke–Coulston–Steeple Ashton–Trowbridge (daily), H6030: Trowbridge–Steeple Ashton–Keevil (daily) extended to Bulkington (weekdays) and through to Worton, Poulshot and Devizes (Tuesdays, Thursdays and Saturdays), and H6031 Devizes–Potterne–Worton (daily). They replaced former L&D licences H4035 (Trowbridge–Devizes), H4036 (Market Lavington–Trowbridge) and Sudweeks licences H3993, 4141 (Devizes–Trowbridge) and H4140 (Devizes–Coulston). However, Bodman continued to run from Devizes to Worton and Trowbridge.

The new network was introduced on 9 December 1937. Licence H6030 emerged as Trowbridge–Bulkington (not Mondays or Wednesdays), extended to Devizes on Thursdays and Saturdays. Licence H6031 ran via Poulshot rather than Potterne. Other changes were:

H1368: Market Lavington–Erlestoke–Bath – withdrawn.
H1369: Codford–Frome was curtailed to start at Warminster rather than Codford in favour of W&D 24.
H4037: Easterton–Market Lavington–Devizes covered Easterton Sands by means of a Thursday and Saturday evening extension to/from Easterton; H4040 covered this small projection, rather than the former separate service.
H4038: Chicklade/Hindon–Salisbury was absorbed into Wilts & Dorset's service 37 between Mere and Salisbury.
H4039: Codford–Salisbury was absorbed into W&D's main service 24 (Salisbury–Warminster–Trowbridge), which was already running every two hours.

H4043: Devizes–Urchfont–Easterton–Market Lavington was reduced to one late evening journey from Devizes on Tuesday, Thursday and Saturday, with the Sunday journeys being shortened and transferred to Wilts & Dorset service 32 (Easterton–Devizes).

H4044: Codford–Devizes was curtailed to start at Warminster rather than Codford, in favour of W&D 24. It also gained a Saturday afternoon journey from Imber to Warminster and a Saturday evening return facility from Warminster to Devizes that also allowed Imber folk to get back from Warminster at 5 p.m. This incorporated C. S. White's Imber–Warminster service.

Thus, the former L&D service network began to alter and contract, although the premises at Market Lavington were to be used for a short time longer. However, the BTMC board meeting on 25 February 1938 considered the acquisition of a site at 12 Market Place, Devizes, as a location for a new garage, office and waiting room. This also bordered on Station Road, and the garage was under construction by spring 1938, opening later that year, whereupon the Market Lavington premises could be vacated, truly signifying the end of an era. Harry Hobbs maintained his connection with buses, being appointed as BTMC's Market Lavington parcel agent, at his shop in the High Street. Bruce Gale was asked to go to Devizes to take charge and could have occupied a flat over the new offices. For some reason, he decided not to go and was out of work for six months, with the family having to move to Bromham to live with one set of grandparents. Walter (Wally) Edward Doel became BTMC's local manager in Devizes. In June 1938 it was noted that Ivydene had been rented to a Mr J. Cartwright at £50 per year. By early 1940 it was unoccupied, and it was requisitioned by the War Department from 31 March that year for use as local headquarters by various batteries forming part of searchlight regiments of the Royal Artillery. Bruce Gale eventually got a job in the office of Frank Chivers & Son in Devizes. Frank Chivers was not involved with the main family business, and as well as being a coal and potato merchant, he had some fields where he kept cattle. By 1939, the Gale family were back in Market Lavington, living at Spin Hill.

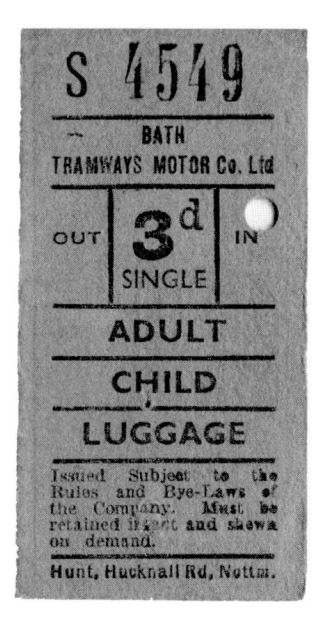

A selection of tickets issued by Bath Tramways Motor Co. Ltd.

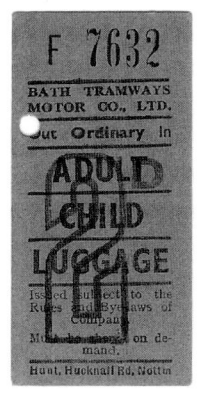

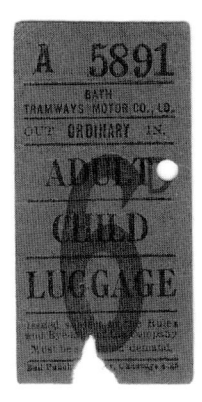

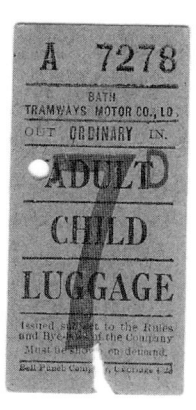

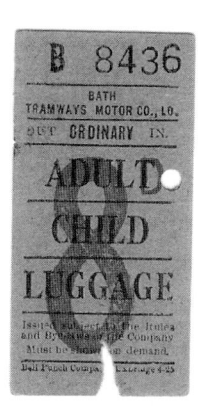

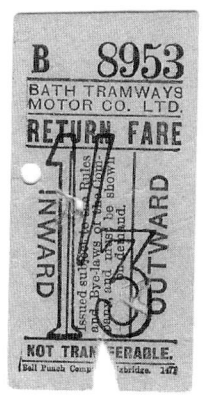

Afterwards: A Selective Miscellany

Although Lavington & Devizes Motor Services had been quietly laid to rest in the spring of 1937, it may be worthwhile to explore some of the subsequent happenings, ending with a brief comment on a few remaining vestiges of the Sayer legacy in the present day.

After selling their shares in L&DMS to BTMC in 1932, the Chivers brothers continued with their various business enterprises. Among the building projects that W. E. Chivers & Sons was involved with, or was principal contractor for, were tank barracks at Perham Down and Warminster in 1935–7, wartime military installations, rebuilding of bomb-damaged properties, and new post-war houses – ranging from prefabs in Hillworth Road in Devizes to locations in South Wales. In 1946 Chivers won the contract for the creation of the Atomic Energy Research Establishment at the RAF airfield at Harwell, which started out with a value of £150,000 but subsequently grew into £20 million worth of work; the firm was on this site for almost forty years and they also gained contracts for work at Aldermaston Atomic Weapons Research Establishment. Although new prestigious work rolled in, overheads were higher and profits lower than they should have been, and the old plant was in need of renewal. For the first time, no dividend was paid to shareholders in 1962, and six years later directors from outside the family were brought in. Bad debts during a recession and a large fall in profits conspired, creating the need for receivers to be called in October 1985. The firm subsequently closed. Their former headquarters in Devizes is where Morrisons supermarket now stands.

As already noted, the former L&DMS premises adjacent to the marketplace in Market Lavington were, in due course, used for other purposes after BTMC relocated their local garage and office to Devizes. After the war, Ivydene was split into four separate residences. The bus garaging area on the north side of the marketplace subsequently became the site for an agricultural engineering works run by A. Wordley & Co., who came to the village in 1950. For a long time, the buildings surrounding the marketplace had been in a poor condition, and by the 1950s had become decrepit. Several had been condemned, and there was confusion as to who exactly owned the title to the properties and the marketplace itself. By the early 1960s, new District

No. 2253 in the BTMC fleet was a Bristol L5G with a thirty-two-seat bus body built in Bristol Tramways' own body works at Brislington. Delivered in 1939, it is seen after the war, possibly inside Devizes garage, labelled for service 36, which ran from Devizes to Chippenham via Calne. (J. Batten Collection)

Council housing had replaced the old maltings and fire station on the west side and the Wordley premises on the north side. Most of the buildings on the eastern side were demolished in 1961, the site being used to relocate Wordley & Co., who became Wiltshire Agricultural Engineering Co. Ltd (WAE) in the mid-1960s. Ivydene was still partially occupied in 1964 but was later demolished and the land subsumed into the WAE premises. In 1990, the whole of the WAE site and its buildings were cleared and redeveloped for housing known as Rochelle Court. The marketplace itself was eventually laid out as a car park, including residential parking for the surrounding properties.

In Bath, the last trams ran on 6 May 1939; the Bath Electric Tramways company, however, continued as a bus operator, for the services that replaced the tram routes, alongside its BTMC subsidiary. The bus services around Devizes being operated by BTMC only saw minor changes up to the outbreak of the Second World War. However, once war had been declared, a number of service reductions or suspensions were introduced by several of the operators, BTMC included, to save fuel, in common with quite a few other areas of the country. As the war progressed, it proved possible to restore some of them. In 1940, BTMC reintroduced a service numbering regime; those for the former L&DMS territory, reflecting what was running at that time, were:

Another member of BTMC's 1938 trio of AEC Regal/Weymann coaches was 2249, seen in Bath while operating the Salisbury service via Devizes on a murky, damp day during the Second World War, as evidenced by the masked headlamps. (J. Batten Collection)

36: Devizes–Calne–Chippenham
36A: Devizes–Studley–Chippenham
37: Devizes–All Cannings (extended through to Pewsey on Sundays)
39: Devizes–Erlestoke–Trowbridge
40: Trowbridge–Bulkington (extended through to Devizes on Thursdays)
41: Devizes–Market Lavington–Easterton
42 Imber–Warminster (Saturdays only)
43: Warminster–Frome (Wednesdays, but suspended)
50: Bath–Wormwood or Corsham–Melksham–Devizes–Salisbury

Some points of interest surrounding later changes include those to services 42 and 43. The latter, when reinstated after the war, was curtailed to start at Longbridge Deverill; it only lasted for another few months. In 1943, the military authority that owned much of the surrounding land, as well as being the landlord of most of the properties in Imber, decided that it also required the village itself, so its buildings could be used to train American troops in the art of house-to-house fighting, prior to the D-Day Landings. The inhabitants were compulsorily and controversially evacuated, for the good of the war effort, just before Christmas, having been given a few weeks' notice. This was on the assumption that they could return to live there again once the area was no longer required for military purposes. The village's name was effectively removed from the map, and they have never been able to do so. Thus, BTMC service 42 was withdrawn in December 1943 and the road through the village closed off.

Judging by the military uniforms and fashions, this poor-quality but interesting view of Market Lavington's marketplace was taken during the Second World War or shortly afterwards. At the back of the marketplace are the old L&DMS premises, abandoned since 1938 when BTMC opened their new Devizes garage. The old boarded-up windows surviving from the original house still show the faded words 'Travel by Bus' and 'Travel by Coach'. To its right is the start of Northbrook, and the access point to the original L&DMS garage behind Ivydene. (MLM)

In 1951, Bristol Tramways transferred five Bristol G05G double-deckers from the Gloucester City Services fleet to BTMC. They had been rebuilt with Bristol K-type radiators and lowbridge bodywork by Longwell Green. No. 3907 is at the Salisbury terminus of service 50 from Bath via Devizes, in New Canal. (J. Batten Collection)

In later years, after much protest, the Ministry of Defence allowed access to the road through deserted and battle-scarred Imber on certain days each year, but for one's own safety one may not stray away from the roadway due to unexploded munitions. The parish church of St Giles is still maintained, and holds a service on certain occasions. Another activity, once a year, has been the operation of a special bus service from Warminster to Imber, using, in the main, red AEC Routemaster double-deck buses that once ran in London. From 2011, some journeys were extended to run through to the Market Lavington area.

In 1944, the journeys on service 50 that ran via Corsham were renumbered 50A, and curtailed to operate only from Bath to Melksham. In 1955 the 50A was extended to Devizes, while from 1963 it was projected onwards to Market Lavington and Easterton, replacing some of the journeys on service 41. Those service 41 journeys that remained were soon also to be renumbered 50A, in 1965; from 26 June 1966 a few of these were extended from Easterton to Urchfont, crossing the old boundary line with Wilts & Dorset. New town services in Devizes to Brickley Lane Estate and to Hillworth started on 21 September 1958, while the Sunday extension beyond All Cannings of service 37 to Pewsey had ceased by 1962.

The Transport Act 1947 promoted the nationalisation of the main-line railways, the road haulage industry, ports and waterways and as many of the bus operators as possible. The Tilling Group decided to sell to the government, although the British Electric Traction Co. group chose to remain independent. Thus the Tilling companies – Bristol, Western National and Wilts & Dorset included – came under British Transport Commission (Road Transport Executive) control on 1 January 1948. As it had not operated trams or carriages for a considerable time, the somewhat anachronistic title of Bristol Tramways & Carriage Co. Ltd was changed in May 1957 to the more appropriate Bristol Omnibus Co. Ltd. However, the two Bath-based subsidiaries were retained at that time, and since 1951 had been trading under the more succinct Bath Services name.

In June 1959, Bristol Omnibus and Wilts & Dorset started a new joint service from Salisbury to Swindon via Tidworth and Marlborough, originally numbered 709 but renumbered 470 in 1967. This was effectively a linking of Wilts & Dorset service 9 (Salisbury–Marlborough) and Bristol Omnibus Co. service 70 (Marlborough–Swindon). This naturally used Salisbury bus station as its terminal point, and with Bristol Omnibus there, it opened the way for the BTMC service 50 from Bath and Devizes to at last join the 'big boys' at the Endless Street premises. However, a green Lavington & Devizes MS Parcel Agent sign was visible on a shop in New Canal in Salisbury for a considerable time after the company ceased to exist.

Meanwhile, Wilts & Dorset acquired the bus and coach activities of Frederick Lampard of Pewsey from 31 October 1944. These included a service from Pewsey to Devizes via Upavon and Rushall on weekdays and a Thursday service from Burbage to Devizes via Pewsey and Rushall. A widespread service renumbering scheme by W&D in 1945 brought all their Devizes services into a consecutive block, and included: 10 to Upavon and Salisbury (previously 4), 11 to Easterton (previously 32), 12 to Beechingstoke (previously 33) and 15 to Pewsey – the former Lampard service. The latter was soon replaced by an extension of service 12 through Woodborough, Manningford and Wilcot to Pewsey, emulating the former L&D service, albeit by a different intermediate route.

Another of the Bristol G-type double-deckers was 3910, seen at the other end of service 50 at Bath's Grand Parade. These vehicles replaced four 1948 Bristol L6B single decks that had been used virtually exclusively on service 50. (J. Batten Collection)

Of the seventeen vehicles once licensed to L&DMS and still in the BTMC fleet at the time that control passed to Bristol Tramways at the end of 1936, only three of them survived in service beyond 1937, to be withdrawn the following year. These were ADCs MR 9504 and UM 8861 and Commer Invader RG 1411. The remainder of the somewhat eclectic BTMC fleet made up predominantly of AECs of various types and Commer Invaders was, over a period of time starting in summer 1937, replaced by a substantial batch of AEC Regal/ECW single-deckers, followed by batches of Bristol L5G single-deckers and Bristol K5G double-deckers (for tramway replacement) in 1938/9. Post-war new vehicle deliveries were generally of what became the standard Tilling Group intake – chassis by Bristol's own plant, engines by Bristol or Gardner and bodywork by Eastern Coach Works (ECW). Some rolling stock was transferred in from the parent Bristol Tramways company. For example, three Bristol J-type single decks were allocated to the Bath–Devizes–Salisbury service in 1937. These were replaced in 1938 by 2247–9 (GL 5831–3), new AEC Regals with thirty-two-seat bodies by Weymann with coach seats. Some of the Bath-based vehicles were licensed to Bath Electric Tramways Ltd. From 1944, the dark blue and white Bristol/Bath livery (and in some cases a wartime all-over grey livery) began to be replaced by standard Tilling green and cream.

Although there were some changes, as already mentioned, the general pattern of bus service provided by BTMC remained relatively stable until the late 1950s/early 1960s, when falling patronage and rising operating costs saw the need for some reduction. As wages, living standards and disposable income began to rise in the 1950s, after the period of wartime and post-war austerity, there were more private cars on the road, for work, shopping and leisure purposes. Increasing ownership of televisions reduced demand for trips to the cinema. Unfortunately, wage awards resulted in higher operating costs in the bus industry, and thus the need for fare increases. Demand for coach excursions fell too, although there were some additional earning opportunities for bus operators in taking children to and from school each day, as some of the smaller village schools had been closed and (especially) secondary education concentrated on fewer, but larger, sites. In hindsight, it may be said that bus industry management did not adapt quickly enough to the changing socio-economic circumstances. Cutbacks in rural areas, particularly to evening and Sunday services, or a reduction in the number of days a week a service ran, became more noticeable from the mid-1960s onwards.

In order to remove duplication, Bristol Omnibus Co. and its subsidiaries brought in a major service renumbering scheme in 1967. Services in the Devizes area became:

270 Bath–Devizes–Salisbury (previously 50)
271/272 Bath–Devizes–Market Lavington–Easterton (previously 50A/50C)
273/274 Devizes town services (previously 38)
275 Devizes–All Cannings (previously 37)
276 Devizes–Trowbridge (previously 39)
277 Trowbridge–Bulkington/Devizes (previously 40)
278–280 Devizes–Calne–Chippenham (previously 36/36A)
471 Devizes–Swindon (previously 71)

After only a year, the Bristol Gs were replaced on service 50 by new lowbridge Bristol KSWs, with ECW bodies featuring platform doors. No. 8088 (OHY 936) was one of two allocated to Devizes. (J. Batten Collection)

Another Transport Act, first promoted in 1962, led in due course to the break-up of the British Transport Commission. Bus and coach companies administered by the Tilling Association Ltd were put under the control of the Transport Holding Company, and financial links between the subsidiary companies and the Railways Board were severed. The management of Wilts & Dorset Motor Services Ltd was amalgamated with that of Hants & Dorset Motor Services on 1 April 1964, creating a close association. Wilts & Dorset's assets were vested in Hants & Dorset on 1 January 1969, the date when the new National Bus Company (NBC), created by the Transport Act 1968, took over from the Transport Holding Company.

It was not long before NBC regional management undertook some rationalisation of their operating companies. In the South West, this included the full integration of Bath Tramways Motor Co. and Bath Electric Tramways into Bristol Omnibus Co. from 1 January 1970, as there were no longer any political, financial or boundary issues requiring their retention as separate entities. From the same date, the Trowbridge depot and west Wiltshire services of Western National were transferred to Bristol Omnibus, including historic service 238 from Trowbridge to Devizes. Just over two years later, on All Fools Day 1972, the services and vehicles of Wilts & Dorset were subsumed into Hants & Dorset Motor Services Ltd.

Under NBC auspices, changes and reductions to Bristol and Hants & Dorset services, in pursuit of economies, came at frequent intervals in the 1970s and early 1980s as patronage declined further. This involved discussions with, and subsidy support from, Wiltshire County Council. A notable alteration from 4 November 1979 involved service 238 between Devizes and Trowbridge, which was withdrawn and replaced by a diversion of 277 between those towns, via Seend, instead of Poulshot and Worton, which were left to Bodmans. Easterton Sands lost its buses at the same time, with the removal of the few 271 journeys that went there. The last remnants of the former L&DMS Devizes–Pewsey service, Bristol Omnibus service 275 into Devizes from Alton Barnes on Saturdays, passed to Bodmans Coaches in October 1981, while the Thursday journeys passed to Brownings Coaches of Box. The Bath–Devizes–Salisbury services were recast at the same time to include the extension of some 271/272 journeys through to Salisbury, after detouring via Market Lavington and Easterton and then retracing their route back to West Lavington crossroads.

In preparation for the eventual privatisation of the National Bus Co., some of the larger subsidiaries began to be broken up into smaller units. A large section of Bristol Omnibus was separated out into a new Cheltenham & Gloucester Omnibus Co. Ltd on 11 September 1983, including the Swindon area where it traded as Swindon & District. Similarly, the Wiltshire, eastern Dorset and south-west Hampshire parts of Hants & Dorset Motor Services had been separated and renamed, somewhat sentimentally, Wilts & Dorset Bus Co. Ltd from 1 April 1983. The 'country' (i.e. non-Bristol city) area of Bristol Omnibus began to trade as Badgerline in 1985, prior to the activation of a separate company – Badgerline Ltd – from 1 January 1986. A new green and yellow livery was adopted for the vehicles. Later in the year, the company was sold to its management team, led by Trevor Smallwood.

The Transport Act 1985, which provided for the privatisation of the NBC, also promoted the 'deregulation' of the bus industry. Road Service licensing, together with

Probably as a result of a failure of a BTMC vehicle at Salisbury, Wilts & Dorset occasionally came to the rescue by supplying a vehicle for a round trip to Bath on service 50. This rare view shows Wilts & Dorset Bristol KSW6B No. 393 (KHR 530) a long way from home, in Bath. (L. Tancock Collection)

This Bristol LS bus of Bath Services is operating route 41 from Easterton to Devizes via Market Lavington – part of which of course had been Fred Sayer's very first service. (L. Tancock Collection)

The Bristol K double-deckers were replaced in due course at Devizes by Bristol Lodekka variants, including Bath Services 8496 (856 CHU) of 1959, a LD6G model with fifty-eight-seat bodywork by ECW. It is leaving Devizes garage in Station Road, ready to work service 50A which ran from Bath to Easterton via Melksham, Devizes and Market Lavington; this eventually replaced local service 41. (R. F. Mack)

the tedious process of Traffic Court hearings and frustration created by refusals to license due to objections, was abolished, and it merely became necessary to register one's introduction, change or cancellation of a bus service by applying to the traffic commissioner at least forty-two days in advance of the start date. Once operators had identified what they wished to run on a commercial basis, without local authority financial support, it was then left to the latter to plan, competitively tender and fund such additional facilities as they could afford, as deemed socially necessary. The concepts of blanket revenue support for loss-making bus services and cross-subsidisation, in theory, had to be abandoned.

The 'deregulation' part of the Act became effective on 26 October 1986. Around Devizes, commercial opportunities and award of contracts resulted in more work for the smaller operators such as Bodmans, Devizes Taxis, Melksham Coaches and Tourist Coaches. Wilts & Dorset finally withdrew from Urchfont, with school journeys continuing with Devizes Taxis, while local interests established the Urchfont Community Bus, with volunteer drivers. On weekdays they ran into Devizes and introduced monthly or twice-monthly trips to Swindon, Salisbury and Bath. Melksham Coaches gained some journeys on the Devizes–Trowbridge services from Badgerline, while the latter's offering on the Bath–Devizes corridor was largely consolidated as just service 272, which continued to run through to Market Lavington and Easterton. The trunk Devizes–Salisbury service (renumbered 23) passed under a contract to a small

Deep in the Wiltshire countryside is Bristol Omnibus Co. 2950, a Bristol MW with ECW bodywork. Service 275 from Devizes to All Cannings was previously BTMC service 37, and a remnant of the Lavington & Devizes Motor Services route from Pewsey. Today, much of the area is covered by the demand-responsive Connect to Wiltshire ('C2W') services, funded and administered by Wiltshire Council. While parts of some services run to a timetable, for many small communities, the bus only comes now if you telephone to book a journey! (J. Batten Collection)

Typical of Tilling-group standard single-deck buses of the late 1950s/early 1960s is this Bristol MW of Bristol Omnibus Co., working a service 270 journey to Devizes. (P. Sposito)

independent firm – Coombe Hill Coaches, although the bulk of their activity lasted only until early June 1987, after which Wilts & Dorset secured the main contract as an expansion of their service 2. From August 1988 until October 1990, there was actually competition on the Salisbury route between Wilts & Dorset and an operator that called itself, grandiosely, Tidworth Silver Star, owned by Messrs Dennett and Jones.

Thereafter and continuing to the present day, bus service alterations, renumbering, reductions and changes of operator in western Wiltshire have continued on a never-ending basis, as contracts changed hands every few years (or, in some cases, months), as commercial providers found it necessary to adjust their networks and as the County Council struggled to work within a smaller budget.

The Wilts & Dorset Bus Co. Ltd was sold to its management team on 24 June 1987 and remained in their hands until it became part of the Go Ahead Group in August 2003. In 1995, Badgerline Holdings joined with Grampian Transport from Aberdeen, the latter being led by Moir Lockhead. Thus was formed FirstBus PLC, which was to become the largest bus operator in the UK. The operating entity of Badgerline Ltd was later changed to First Bristol Buses Ltd, which was renamed First Somerset & Avon Ltd on 30 May 2003.

At the time of writing, the former L&DMS service between Devizes, West Lavington, Shrewton and Salisbury is still operated regularly by Wilts & Dorset, numbered 2. Most journeys divert between Potterne and West Lavington to serve Market Lavington, but approach via Grove Road, before turning west on to The Spring, thus missing the centre of the village. APL Travel from Crudwell runs service 33 from Devizes to

Moving forward in time, this Bristol LH6L (No. 380) of 1976, leaving Devizes garage in the late 1970s, is representing the era of National Bus Co. (NBC) ownership of Bristol Omnibus. NBC subsidiaries were obliged to paint their buses either 'poppy red' or 'leaf green', with Bristol Omnibus using the latter. (P. Sposito)

Seen in Bath labelled for service 272 to Salisbury via Market Lavington, Bristol VRT No. 5600 (JNU 136N) shows the abbreviated 'Bath' fleet name used for a time, as well as Badgerline titles and logo above the lower deck windows, dating this view to the mid-1980s. (P. Sposito)

Waiting in Devizes to continue its journey to Easterton on 10 July 1997 is Badgerline 3536, a Leyland National previously owned by Midland Red West, one of a pair acquired by Badgerline in 1989. (M. Wadman)

In due course, the Badgerline Badger logo appeared prominently on their attractive green and yellow buses. In May 1997, Plaxton Pointer-bodied Dennis Dart No. 240, dating from 1995, was in Devizes, working a service largely a descendant of Fred Sayer's pioneering network some eighty years previously. (M. Wadman)

Before First Somerset & Avon's presence in Devizes became minimal, their service X72 worked daily from Bath to Market Lavington and Easterton, although the section east of Devizes was renumbered 272/273 in June 2008. On 18 May 2006, their Volvo B10BLE No. 62238 (Y947 CSF), with Wright bodywork, pauses in Devizes marketplace. This bus had come from Scottish operator Midland Bluebird within the First group. What a contrast to Fred Sayer's vehicles! (M. Wadman)

Chippenham through Bromham and Calne. Much of the area to the east of Devizes once covered by the L&D and Wilts & Dorset Pewsey services now sees the demand-responsive 'Connect2Wiltshire' services. Of all the local independent operators active in the 1920s and 1930s, only Bodman of Worton survived until recently, latterly trading as Wiltshire Buses and controlled by the Hatts Coaches business of Foxham, owned by the Hillier family. Sadly, Hatts/Bodman ceased trading for financial reasons in July 2014, just as this book was being finalised.

A significant event in September 2010 saw Monday–Saturday First services 271–273 curtailed on a commercial basis to only operate between Bath and Melksham (Bowerhill). This prompted Fosseway Coaches (also known as Faresaver) of Chippenham to step in and extend their competing X72 Bath–Melksham service to Devizes. This connected with a bidirectional loop service numbered X71, via Urchfont, Easterton, Market Lavington, West Lavington crossroads and Potterne. The two services were later combined as X72. The only remaining First operation in the Devizes area is currently the extension of a few contracted evening journeys and the Sunday journeys on 271/272 to Devizes and on to Market Lavington, Easterton and Urchfont. Thus the direct lineage of operators – from Lavington & Devizes MS, to Bath Tramways Motor Co., to Bristol Omnibus, to Badgerline, to First Bristol Buses, to First Somerset & Avon – is now restricted to these few journeys.

To fully describe the history of all the bus services that have served Devizes or have run over parts of Fred Sayer's route network from 1937 until the present day would require several more books, and those are other stories for another day.

Compared to past views, today's marketplace in Market Lavington looks totally different. With one exception, all the buildings from Fred Sayer's time have gone, replaced by new housing. At the back, bungalows stand on the site of the L&DMS garage. In fact, nothing structural now remains to remind us of L&DMS and all the public transport activity from 1915 to 1938. (Author)

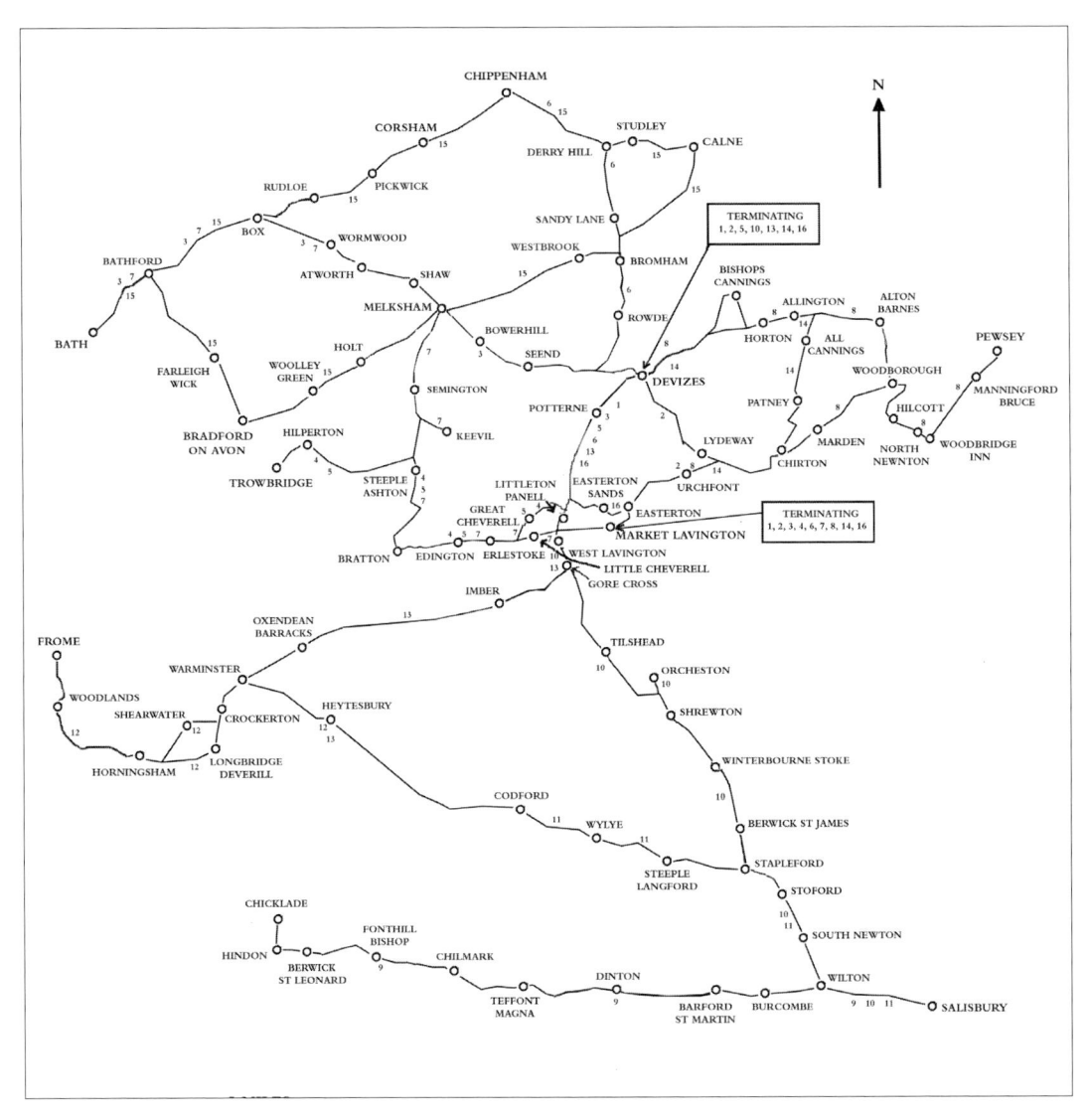

Bus services of Lavington & Devizes Motor Services at various times (except Tidworth–Andover service). The numbers are for identification purposes only and refer to services detailed in Appendix 1, opposite.

Appendix 1

Bus Services of F. H. Sayer and Lavington & Devizes Motor Services Ltd (L&DMS) 1915–37 (Also Successor Bath Tramways Motor Co. Ltd (BTMC) Services to End of 1937)

Also given are the initial L&DMS Southern traffic area road service licence numbers allocated in June 1931 (prefixed J), and the later Western traffic area numbers (prefixed H).

(The map codes referred to below correspond to the numbers shown on the map on the opposite page.)

Market Lavington–Devizes via Potterne (J1342, H4037, map code 1)
By 5/15 (?): Market Lavington–West Lavington crossroads–Littleton Panell–Black Dog–Potterne Wick–Potterne–Mount Pleasant–Devizes (daily except Wednesday): acquired from Bath Electric Tramways Ltd
12/6/21: Introduced also on Wednesday
5/26: BTMC timetable booklet showed no Sunday journeys on the 'local' service (route covered by Market Lavington–Devizes–Bath service), but seemingly only for a short period, before Market Lavington–Devizes 'local' journeys via Potterne on Sundays were once again shown
By late 1931: Believed extended from Market Lavington to Easterton at least on Thursday and Saturday
By 28/11/32: Extended daily from Market Lavington to Easterton
11/10/34: Some journeys diverted at West Lavington crossroads to serve West Lavington village and 'The Gun' (junction of A360/Rutts Lane)
5/37: Road service licence applied for by Bath Tramways Motor Co. Ltd (BTMC)

Market Lavington–Devizes via Urchfont (J1356, H4043, map code 2)
By 5/15(?): Market Lavington–Easterton–Urchfont–Lydeway–Stert Turn–Devizes (Sunday): acquired from Bath Electric Tramways Ltd
By 1926: Also a Saturday morning journey from Market Lavington to Devizes until at least spring 1931 but not by 1934
c. 7/36: Operated Monday–Saturday late afternoon/evening, and Sunday
5/37: Road service licence applied for by BTMC

3/12/37: Service passed to Wilts & Dorset Motor Services Ltd (W&D) as part of their service 32 Easterton–Devizes, except for one Tuesday/Thursday/Saturday evening journey from Devizes, retained by BTMC

Market Lavington–Salisbury
11/15: Market Lavington–Easterton–Urchfont–Lydeway–Stert Turn–Devizes–Mount Pleasant–Potterne–Potterne Wick–Black Dog–Littleton Panell–West Lavington–Salisbury (Tuesday)
By 1920: Believed withdrawn

Market Lavington–Bath via Devizes (J1352, H2961, map code 3)
11/15: Market Lavington–West Lavington crossroads–Littleton Panell–Black Dog–Potterne Wick–Potterne–Mount Pleasant–Devizes–Seend–Bowerhill–Melksham–Shaw–Atworth–Wormwood–Box–Bathford–Bath (Wednesday)
1/11/20: Sayer also operated on Monday and Saturday. Also a round trip from Bath to Devizes on Thursday, operated by BTMC
12/6/21: Sayer operated to Bath daily except Thursday
By 2/22: BTMC also operating Devizes–Melksham on Thursday and Bath–Devizes on Sunday
By 11/22: L&DMS service to Bath operated daily. BTMC also operating a round trip to Devizes from Bath on Monday, Tuesday, Wednesday and Friday afternoons – withdrawn by 2/24
10/27: BTMC journeys numbered 13 (until 1934)
9/1/33: Bath–Devizes section of route joined to Devizes–Salisbury service, although the two sections were still advertised separately. Journeys from/to Market Lavington operated only when buses commenced from or returned to the depot. Road service licences still shared between BTMC and L&DMS, but generally using vehicles licensed to BTMC, which ran 'on hire' to L&DMS when on journeys or sections of route licensed to the latter
5/37: Road service licence for L&DMS journeys applied for by BTMC

Market Lavington–Trowbridge (J1343, H4036, map code 4)
14/6/21: Market Lavington–West Lavington crossroads–Little Cheverell–Erlestoke–Tinhead–Edington–Bratton–Steeple Ashton–Hilperton–Trowbridge (Tuesday/Thursday/Saturday)
By 2/22: Operating Monday to Saturday
By 11/22: Also operating on Sunday (via Great Cheverell)
By 7/29: Whole service operating via Great Cheverell
5/37: Road service licence applied for by BTMC

Trowbridge–Devizes (J1355, H4035, map code 5)
16/6/21: Trowbridge–Hilperton–Steeple Ashton–Bratton–Edington–Tinhead–Erlestoke–Great Cheverell–Black Dog–Potterne Wick–Potterne–Mount Pleasant–Devizes (Thursday)
By 11/32: Also operating Great Cheverell–Devizes on schooldays and Saturday evening
5/37: Road service licence applied for by BTMC

Market Lavington–Chippenham (J1353, H4041, map code 6)
17/6/21: Market Lavington–West Lavington crossroads–Littleton Panell–Black Dog–Potterne Wick–Potterne–Mount Pleasant–Devizes–Rowde–Bell Inn–Bromham–Sandy Lane–Derry Hill–Swan Inn–Chippenham (Friday)
By 9/23: Operating also on Tuesday and Saturday
After 1927 but by 4/29: Operated daily from Devizes but certain journeys ran through from/to Market Lavington on Saturday/Sunday
c. 11/33: Journeys from/to Market Lavington operated alternate Fridays and Sunday

c. 7/36: Journeys from/to Market Lavington withdrawn

5/37: Road service licence applied for by BTMC

Market Lavington–Bath via Erlestoke (J1348, H1368, map code 7)

31/8/21: Market Lavington–West Lavington crossroads–Little Cheverell–Erlestoke–Tinhead–Edington–Bratton–Steeple Ashton–Keevil–Semington–Melksham–Shaw–Atworth–Box–Bathford–Bath (Wednesday)

By 9/23: Also operating on Saturdays

By 11/32: Diverted to operate via Great Cheverell

5/37: Road service licence applied for by BTMC

Market Lavington–Devizes via Woodborough, later Pewsey–Devizes (J1345, H4235, map code 8)

By Autumn 1921: Market Lavington–Easterton–Urchfont–Chirton–Marden–Woodborough–Alton Barnes–Stanton St Bernard turn–All Cannings–Allington–Horton–Devizes (Tuesday/Thursday/Saturday)

24/4/22: Revised to commence from Pewsey via Manningford Bruce–Woodbridge Inn–North Newnton–Hilcot–Bottlesford to Woodborough, then as before to Devizes (Monday–Saturday)

By 11/22: Also operating on Sunday, but withdrawn on Wednesday except for a through round trip from Pewsey to Bath via Devizes

By 12/26: Through journey to Bath withdrawn, and Pewsey–Devizes service reduced to operate Thursday/Saturday/Sunday

By 9/3/33: Woodbridge Inn–Devizes section increased to operate daily. Diverted between Horton and Devizes via Bishops Cannings

By 5/36: Whole service reduced again to Thursday/Saturday/Sunday

5/37: Road service licence applied for by BTMC

Hindon–Salisbury (J1346, H4038, map code 9)

8/1/23: Hindon–Berwick St Leonard–Fonthill Bishop–Ridge Cottages–Chilmark–Teffont Magna–Dinton–Barford St Martin–Burcombe–Ugford–Wilton–Salisbury (Tuesday/Saturday): acquired from C. E & C. H. Hall

By 1926: Operating daily

c. 9/35: Extended to start and finish at Chicklade on Tuesdays

5/37: Road service licence applied for by BTMC

3/12/37: Transferred to W&D as part of service 37 Salisbury–Hindon–Mere

Devizes–Salisbury (J1351, H4042, map code 10)

8/1/23: Devizes–Mount Pleasant–Potterne–Potterne Wick–Black Dog–Littleton Panell–West Lavington–Gore Cross–Tilshead–Shrewton–Winterbourne Stoke–Berwick St James–Stapleford–Stoford–South Newton–Wilton–Salisbury (Monday–Saturday). Also journeys from Orcheston via Shrewton and then as above to Salisbury (Tuesday/Saturday): acquired from C. E. & C. H. Hall

By 2/24: Devizes–Salisbury service operating daily

By 7/28: Orcheston journeys operating Monday to Saturday

9/1/33: Combined with Devizes–Bath service (including journeys on BTMC service 13) and operated by BTMC vehicles on hire to L&DMS

5/37: Road service licence for Devizes/Orcheston–Salisbury applied for by BTMC

Codford–Salisbury (J1350, H4039, map code 11)
By 6/25 (probably by sometime in 1924): Codford–Wylye–Steeple Langford–Stapleford–Stoford–South Newton–Wilton–Salisbury (Tuesday/Saturday): acquired from W&D (service 5)
By 1929: Operating also on Sunday
5/37: Road service licence applied for by BTMC
3/12/37: Withdrawn (covered by W&D service 24 Trowbridge–Warminster–Salisbury)

Codford–Frome (J1347, H1369, map code 12)
By 6/25 (probably by sometime in 1924): Codford–Heytesbury–Warminster–Crockerton–Horningsham–Woodlands–Frome (Wednesday): acquired from W&D (service 5B)
c. 1/36: Diverted between Crockerton and Horningsham via Longbridge Deverill
5/37: Road service licence applied for by BTMC
3/12/37: Codford–Warminster section withdrawn (covered by W&D service 24)

Codford–Devizes (J1349, H4044, map code 13)
By 6/25 (probably by sometime in 1924): Codford–Heytesbury–Warminster–Imber–Gore Cross–West Lavington–Littleton Panell–Black Dog–Potterne Wick–Potterne–Mount Pleasant–Devizes (Thursday): acquired from W&D (service 5C)
5/37: Road service licence applied for by BTMC
3/12/37: Codford–Warminster section withdrawn (covered by W&D service 24)

Market Lavington–Devizes via Patney (J1345, H4045, map code 14)
By 1926: Market Lavington–Easterton–Urchfont–Chirton–Patney–All Cannings–Allington–Horton–Devizes (schooldays)
5/37: Road service licence applied for by BTMC

Calne–Bath (Map code 15)
By 1926 (11/7/25?): Calne–Sandy Lane–Westbrook–Melksham–Broughton Gifford turn–Holt–Woolley Green–Bradford-on-Avon–Farleigh Wick–Bathford–Bath (Tuesday/Wednesday/Friday/Saturday)
Calne–Studley–Swan Inn–Chippenham–Corsham–Pickwick–Rudloe–Box–Bathford–Bath (Sunday)
L&DMS believed to have operated these BTMC services (BTMC Nos 8 and 9 respectively from 1927). BTMC later operated journeys on service 8 on Sunday and service 9 Monday–Saturday
By 8/30 (?): Withdrawn by L&DMS and wholly operated by BTMC

Market Lavington–Devizes via Easterton Sands (J1344, H4040, map code 16)
6/31: Market Lavington–Easterton–Easterton Sands–Black Dog–Potterne Wick–Potterne–Mount Pleasant–Devizes (Thursday and Saturday evening): a road service licence was applied for, to continue the service started previously at an unknown date
c. 7/36: Saturday evening service replaced by an extension of the main Easterton–Devizes service from/to Easterton Sands
5/37: Road service licence applied for by BTMC

Tidworth–Andover (J1354)
6/31: Tidworth–Ludgershall–Biddleston House–Redenham–Appleshaw–Weyhill–Andover: a road service licence was applied for, to continue the service started previously at an unknown date
?/?: Withdrawn (road service licence not granted?)

Appendix 2

List of Vehicles Known to Have Been Operated by Lavington & Devizes Motor Services

The list has been compiled from data collected by Roger Grimley, Andrew Waller, Geoff Bruce and others, which contained discrepancies relating to certain vehicles. As will be noted, there are uncertainties, but further details are lacking.

The 'Date In' given for vehicles with second-hand chassis, or those assembled from components or spare parts from 1921 onwards, is generally the date of first registration in Wiltshire.

The * symbol next to the registration number denotes a vehicle believed to have been in stock in May 1932, when control of the company passed to Bath Tramways Motor Co. Ltd.

The 'B' symbol adjacent to 'Date Out' indicates that ownership was transferred at that date to Bath Tramways Motor Co. Ltd. For BTMC fleet numbers allocated in December 1936, see text.

Where possible, the standard codes as recognised in most enthusiasts' publications have been used to describe body types and seating capacities:

Prefix:
B: Single-deck bus
C: Single-deck coach, including 'all-weather' type with side windows, folding canvas roof for the main part and conventional seating and entrances
Ch: Charabanc with folding canvas hood, usually with individual door to each row of seats.
Figures: Seating capacity as shown

Suffix:
D: Dual entrance
F: Front or forward entrance
R: Rear entrance

Fleet No.	Registration	Chassis Manufacturer	Body Manufacturer	Body Type & Seating	Year Chassis New	Date In	Date Out	Note
	AM 4980	Overland 40 cwt		Ch14	1915	9/18	?	
	FB 028	Commer WP2		Ch22	1912	4/19	?	1
7	HR 655	Commer RC/Sayer	Dodson/Bath E.T./Sayer	B32F	1917	c/19	/27	2
	HR 2587*	Crossley 20/24hp		B14	1920	8/20	?	3
1	AM 9059	Commer WP1		Ch28	1914	1/21	/29	4
	AM 9447	Commer WP1		Ch28	1913	1/21	9/22	4
5	AM 9698	Commer RC		Ch28	1913	1/21	2/29	4
	AM 8797	Commer RC		Ch or B	?	2/21	?	4
	AM 9699	Commer WP1		Ch32	1913	3/21	By 3/27	4
2	HR 4065	Commer WP1/ L&DMS		Ch26	1921	4/21	6/24	5
	AM 6491	Commer RC		Ch32 or B32	1918	5/21	/27	4,6
	HR 4870	Crossley X/L&DMS		Ch14	1921	6/21	?	
11	HR 5027	Crossley X		Ch14	1918	7/21	By 10/30	7
12	HR 5028	Crossley X		Ch14	1918	7/21	By 8/30	7
	HR 5072	Commer RC		B26	1918	7/21	6/23	7,8
	HR 5895	Commer RC		B32	1918	1/22	12/23	7
	HR 6666	Commer RC		B32	1917	5/22	By 1/28	5,7
	HR 6676	Crossley X		Ch14	1918	5/22	By 2/31	7
20	HR 7537	Crossley X/L&DMS		Ch14	1922	11/22	1/29	9
	HR 7538*	Crossley X/L&DMS		Ch14	1922	11/22	10/33B	9
	AM 8761	Commer RC		B32	1917	1/23	3/32	7
24	AM 9371	AEC YC		Ch32	1919	1/23	6/24	10
	AM 9574	AEC YC		Ch32	1919	1/23	/29	
	HR 89	AEC YC		B32	1919	1/23	By 5/32	
	HR 170	AEC YC		Ch32	1919	1/23	?	10
29	HR 1004	Daimler CK		Ch26	1918	1/23	?	11
	HR 5593	Dennis 40hp	Dodson	B32F	1921	1/23	12/26	
10	HR 8651	Crossley X/L&DMS		Ch14	1923	5/23	1/29	7
31	LX 8276*	AEC YC		Ch	1918	5/23	1/35B	12
	FB 051	Commer WP1	Dodson/Bath E.T.	B27D	1916	6/23	12/24	13
	FB 045	Commer WP1	Commer	Ch27	1914	7/23	11/26	14
	MR 58*	AEC YC		C26	1917	1/24	11/34	15
	MR 862	AEC/L&DMS		C32	1924	5/24	9/30	16
	MR 863	AEC/L&DMS		C32	1924	5/24	10/30	16
3	MR 865	AEC/L&DMS		C28	1924	5/24	12/36B	16,17

Appendix 2 125

Fleet No.	Registration	Chassis Manufacturer	Body Manufacturer	Body Type & Seating	Year Chassis New	Date In	Date Out	Notes
1	XM 867*	AEC Y/L&DMS		C28	1922	5/24	12/36B	18
	MR 2468	AEC/L&DMS		B32	1924	1/25	?	16
16	MR 2469	AEC/L&DMS		B32	1924	1/25	12/31	16,19
	MR 3575*	AEC/L&DMS		C28	1925	6/25	12/36B	16, 17
	MR 3576	AEC/L&DMS		C32	1925	6/25	?	16
	L 6476	AEC YA		B28	1920	1/26	?	
	MR 5675	Crossley X/L&DMS		B14	1925	1/26	?	20
	MR 5600	AEC/L&DMS		B32	1925	1/26	1/29	16, 19
	MR 5601	AEC/L&DMS		B32	1925	1/26	1/29	16
	MO 2406*	Fiat 15TER		B20R	1923	/26	5/33B	21
4	LU 9166	AEC YC		Ch or C	1918	?	/31	
	HU 3245*	Reo Speedwagon F		C	?	?	9/32	
8	HF 1743	AEC YC	Hora	B32R	1919	2/27	8/31	
	MR 9504*	ADC 416A	Brush	B32F	1927	6/27	1/34B	22
	NR 3128	AEC Y type		B	?	?	?	23
	MW 1577	AEC Y/L&DMS	Dodson	B32	?	3/28	10/31	24
	MW 4568*	Chevrolet LP		C14	1929	5/29	9/32	
	HR 9981	Chevrolet B		C14	1924	4/30	?	
	MW 7482*	AEC Y/L&DMS		C32	?	6/30	8/32	25
	XV 6211*	Chevrolet	Thurgood	B14F	1928	7/30	?B	26
12	MW 7726*	Lancia Pentaiota	Heaver	B20F	1930	7/30	?	27
	MW 7727*	Lancia Pentaiota	Heaver	B20F	1930	7/30	6/34B	
	MW 7728*	Lancia Pentaiota	Heaver	B20F	1930	7/30	6/34B	
	MW 8248*	Lancia Pentaiota	Heaver	B20F	1931	1/31	?	
	WV 521*	Gilford 168SD	Wycombe	B26F	1928	12/31	12/36B	28
6	YV 3926*	ADC 416A	Hall Lewis	B28F	1928	12/31	1/34B	
21	YV 3927*	ADC 416A	Hall Lewis	B28F	1928	12/31	1/34B	
	UM 8861*	ADC 416A	John Taylor	B32D	1927	3/32	1/34B	
30	FG 4422	AEC 426	Cowieson	B32F	1928	By 7/32	1/34B	
12	FG 4886	AEC 426	Dodson (?)	B32F	1929	By 7/32	12/36B	
	DR 719	AEC 414	Plymouth C.T.	B26F	1926	8/32	1/34B	
13	DR 1215	AEC 414	Plymouth C.T.	B26F	1927	9/32	1/34B	
	DR 1217	AEC 414	Plymouth C.T.	B26F	1927	9/32	1/34B	
	DR 1220	AEC 414	Plymouth C.T.	B26F	1927	9/32	1/34B	
	RG 1316	Commer Invader 6TK	Walker (?)	B20F	1930	9/32	12/36B	
33	RG 1411	Commer Invader 6TK	Walker (?)	B20F	1930	9/32	12/36B	
32	VT 6172	Commer Invader 6TK	?	C20F	1931	4/33	12/36B	

Immediate former operator (as known or recorded):
AM 4980: Grant, Winterbourne Stoke
AM 9371/9574, HR 89/170/1004/5593: Hall, Orcheston
FB 045/051: Bath Tramways Motor Co.
L6476: South Wales Commercial Motors
MO 2406: Denham, Newbury
HF 1743: Wallasey Corporation
HR 9981: Alexander, Lydeway
XV 6211: Wilts & Dorset Motor Services
YV 3926/3927: Samuelson, London, SW1
UM 8861: Hurton, Retford
FG 4422/4886: W. Alexander, Falkirk
DR 719/1215/1217/1220: Plymouth City Transport
RG 1316/1411: River Dee Coaches, Aberdeen
VT 6172: Buckley & Cookson, Basford

Explanation of notes:

1. Originally a Bath Electric Tramways charabanc, requisitioned 1914, acquired by Sayer from the War Department (or from BET), most likely as a chassis only.
2. Body acquired from Bath Electric Tramways (previously on Commer WP1, registered FB 032 or FB 033) and rebuilt by Sayer.
3. Described as canvas-covered van, but may have been used as a passenger vehicle in the early years.
4. Chassis second hand, or from previous owner(s), probably acquired from War Department.
5. Also recorded as Ch32.
6. Also recorded by one source as AM 5491.
7. Chassis acquired from the War Department.
8. Recorded as rebuilt to Ch28.
9. Chassis probably second hand.
10. Re-bodied either while with Halls or L&DMS as a saloon bus with similar capacity.
11. Chassis acquired by Halls from the War Department in 1920.
12. Chassis from a London South Western Railway lorry.
13. Given a B32R body, possibly ex-Wilts & Dorset.
14. Photographed carrying a lorry body at one point.
15. Chassis from a lorry of Chivers, Devizes.
16. AEC Y chassis rebuilt by L&DMS, using AEC components.
17. Re-bodied Dodson B26F, body acquired from Wilts & Dorset in 1929.
18. Former lorry chassis, re-bodied Dodson B28F (after 4/30) with body acquired from Wilts & Dorset in 1929.
19. Also recorded as B26F.
20. Rebuilt chassis.
21. Converted to a lorry 7/31.

Appendix 2

22. Re-bodied later Wycombe B32F by BTMC.
23. Registered in Leicestershire in 1923, acquired from Aldridge (Dealer). Chassis possibly ex-War Department.
24. Reconditioned second-hand chassis with body acquired from Wilts & Dorset.
25. Reconditioned second-hand chassis.
26. Had been used by Wilts & Dorset as a 'baggage van'.
27. Also recorded by one source as MW 7729.
28. Second-hand chassis given a second-hand body (from two different unknown sources)

Another AEC Y type (AY 6650) was acquired from Aldridge (dealer), possibly in chassis form, at around the same time as NR 3128 – its status with L&DMS is not known – it could have been used for the construction of MW 1577 or MW 7482 (?). L&DMS also acquired MR 1393, AEC 202 chassis (new 1924) from Wilts & Dorset 6/32, subsequently used as a basis for a lorry by BTMC.

Bibliography

Chislett, S., *Buses and Trams of Bath* (Millstream Books, 1986)

Crawley, R. J., MacGregor, D. R. and Simpson, F. D., *The Years Between Vol. 1 – The National Omnibus & Transport Co.* (MacGregor, 1979)

Crawley, R. J. and Simpson, F. D., *The Years Between Vol. 3 – Western and Southern National* (Calton Promotions, 1990)

Grimley, R., *Early Motor Bus Services from Salisbury – Upper Avon Valley* (Grimley, 2005)

Grimley, R., *Early Motor Bus Services from Salisbury – Nadder Valley* (Grimley, 2007)

Maggs, C., *The Bath Tramways* (Oakwood Press, 1992)

McGill, B., *Village under the Plain – The Story of Market Lavington* (Bedeguar Books, 2009)

Morris, C., *Western National Omnibus Co.* (Ian Allan, 2008)

Morris, C. and Waller, A., *The Definitive History of Wilts & Dorset Motor Services Ltd* (Hobnob Press, 2006)